INSOLVENCY AND FINANCIAL DISTRESS

How to avoid it and survive it

Brian Finch

BLOOMSBURY

First published in Great Britain 2012

Bloomsbury Publishing Plc
50 Bedford Square
London WC1B 3DP

www.acblack.com
www.bloomsbury.com

A CIP record for this book is available from the British Library.

ISBN: 978-1-4081-5145-7

This book is produced using paper that is made from wood grown in managed, sustainable forests. It is natural, renewable and recyclable. The logging and manufacturing processes conform to the environmental regulations of the country of origin.

Design by Fiona Pike, Pike Design, Winchester
Typeset by Saxon Graphics Ltd, Derby
Printed in Great Britain by Clays Ltd, St Ives plc

CONTENTS

ACKNOWLEDGEMENTS

I would like to express my thanks to John Briggs, barrister, practising from 3 – 4 South Square, Gray's Inn, who is joint author of *Muir Hunter on Personal Insolvency* and to Sam Talby, who is Business Turnaround & Recovery Partner at Bishop Fleming. They kindly scanned the manuscript for me and have made suggestions for improvement and pointed out errors. Any errors that remain, perhaps because I have overidden their suggestions in order to make the book easier to read, or that I have introduced since are, I trust, small. If there any then I lay absolute claim to them.

At Bloomsbury, I would particularly like to thank my editor, Lisa Carden, and copy-editor Fiona Cairns, who have asked the questions that I missed and have driven me to express myself more clearly.

PREFACE

It is said that despite its many glaring (and occasionally fatal) inaccuracies, **The Hitchhiker's Guide to the Galaxy** *itself has outsold the* **Encyclopedia Galactica** *because it is slightly cheaper, and because it has the words 'DON'T PANIC' in large, friendly letters on the cover.*[1]

Telling a friend that I was writing this book, he responded that it is easy to avoid financial distress and insolvency: all you need to do is make a profit. Well, that's perfectly true, as far as it goes, but many successful business people have tiptoed past the open door of insolvency at some time during their careers. My friend provides an illustration: a successful businessman who has headed large organisations, he has latterly become involved in a family company with great prospects, innovative ideas and impressive products. Yet it has been caught out by a massive reorganisation of its public sector customers, which is likely to stymie new business for an entire year, hitting cash flow hard. Of course they are not sitting still. They are developing new products and income streams to fill the gap and the family shareholders are putting in new money to tide it over. I am convinced that eventually it will be a huge success.

But this example illustrates the fact that good companies as well as weak ones suffer 'character-forming' setbacks. And there are solutions for both types, whether it be raising temporary funding or wholesale reorganisation.

This book provides guidance and ideas for the directors, employees, shareholders and creditors of companies that are in financial difficulties. It takes a practical, business-driven approach: this is not a legal textbook and should not be taken as giving legal advice. The law is complicated, changes rapidly and is very dependent upon the precise facts of each case. Readers whose

---

1 Adams, Douglas (1979). *The Hitchhiker's Guide to the Galaxy.* Pocket Books, p. 3.

companies face financial difficulties should take professional advice to guide them through the details of the legal minefield.

But approach these business problems with a commercial mind. Find business solutions and get professional advice to make them work. Of course many accountants, turnaround specialists and insolvency practitioners do adopt this commercial attitude, looking to save businesses and not just to sell off their dismembered body-parts. In fact, many businesses that are in difficulty can be extricated in one form or another, so do not give up hope too soon: acting quickly will make survival and eventual prosperity more likely.

And if insolvency cannot be avoided, the outcome may be difficult, but is never — unlike the plot of the book quoted above — the literal end of the world and is seldom as bad as you think it will be. So:

DON'T PANIC

Keep calm and we will work through some options.

Although the English legal background is used in this book, most of the business issues discussed are universal and would, broadly, apply anywhere.

INTRODUCTION

What is insolvency?

Insolvency occurs when a 'legal or natural person' cannot pay their debts when they fall due. A natural person is a literal person — you or I — while a legal person is a company, charity or association. This book is about companies, and not personal bankruptcy. A government, though, cannot become bankrupt. It can default on its obligations to pay its debts, just like a company, but it fails the second test of insolvency, which is what happens afterwards. The consequences of insolvency are set out in the laws of the country and, in the United Kingdom, require a company to stop incurring any further liabilities that they cannot meet: that includes not taking on more debt and, generally, ceasing to trade. So while a bankrupt individual or a defaulting country continue to exist even though their ability to borrow again is impaired, an insolvent company will often cease to exist (at least in the form it had before) and its assets will be sold or distributed.

These seem simple ideas but the phrase 'when they fall due' hints at something more complex. For example, is a company insolvent if its directors know it *can* pay a debt but just not until a week after the actual due date? What if the gap is a month or three months? Or suppose the company owns a very valuable asset which can be sold and will realise more than enough money to cover the debt, but the sale probably could not be achieved for some time?

There are large numbers of company insolvencies in the UK. There were 16,000 at the low point in 2004 and they peaked at 26,000 in 2009 before falling back to 23,000 in 2010. They were up again by 4% in the second quarter of 2011. This last peak is substantially below the previous one of 1992, both as a total number and as a percentage of active companies. Nonetheless, these cold numbers represent a great deal of anguish for a lot of people.

Many people are affected by insolvency. Creditors are not paid and may suffer their own financial difficulties as a result; shareholders lose their investments; directors and employees lose their jobs, their hopes, their careers. Insolvency is not painless. We read in the newspapers about companies that fail and then re-emerge, trading under a different name but with the same directors and shareholders. We may imagine they have escaped scot free, and there are, indeed, people who exploit and abuse the system and do just that. Only recently I read in the newspaper of a building company that has been the subject of numerous customer complaints which it has customarily ignored. If these complaints are heading towards court proceedings, the directors simply close the company and start a new one.

Cases like this represent a tiny minority of business failures, however: in the main, those who own a business that has failed have also suffered serious consequences. Nonetheless, insolvency is not the end of the world — it *is* possible to salvage something from the wreckage and to rebuild careers.

This book starts with the importance of recognising you have a problem and what you can do, once you encounter financial difficulty, to avoid insolvency itself. All is not lost, and there are alternatives that may save a business from falling over the precipice. So what do you do as one of the many actors in this drama, as a director, an employee or as a creditor?

I spent some time as a senior executive in large companies before co-founding a retail and Internet business and serving as its finance director and company secretary. This business went through many ups and downs before (in order to escape an onerous lease), we put it into administration and then bought it out again, minus the shop that was threatening to bring down the entire edifice. Therefore, from a financial background, I have personal experience of dealing with creditors and debtors, managing the detail of cash flows and, in the end, of dealing with an insolvency process. So what follows is not just based on my research but on direct experience of negotiating with banks and suppliers, of employing lawyers and trying to persuade insolvency practitioners. I too have suffered the stresses that are described in this book. Nonetheless, although common threads connect all insolvencies, every situation is unique — different people behave differently and this book draws from much wider possibilities than just my own experiences.

CHAPTER 1
KNOWING YOU HAVE A PROBLEM

First of all, it's crucial to recognise that you have a problem. There are four indicators that reveal a company is in choppy financial waters:

1. you are finding it hard to pay your bills on time;
2. you produce forecasts that show a cash flow problem in the future;
3. you have a weak balance sheet, probably with a negative value;
4. you know there is a risk of your financiers withdrawing support.

The first of these demonstrates an immediate problem and is instantly recognisable. It comes in two flavours: 'legal action' and 'not yet'.

Legal action

The 'legal action' test is a pretty clear indicator where one or more creditors has:

• obtained a county court judgement against you;
• issued a statutory demand (for more than £750) that remains unpaid after 21 days;
• started proceedings to wind up your company.

There were more than 200,000 county court judgements obtained in 2006, which demonstrates that suppliers are quite ready to use this mechanism to force customers to pay their bills. Since levels of company liquidations in that year were 18,000 across the UK, it is clear that a judgement does not necessarily mean that a company will fail. If the judgement is not paid within 30 days, however, the creditor can go back to the court and seek a winding-up petition against the company — so the county court judgement tends to concentrate minds on paying the outstanding debt.

A statutory demand is a formal document issued by a creditor, demanding payment. It involves no immediate cost to the creditor, who can easily download an example from the Internet. It constitutes an enhanced threat — it strongly implies the issue of a winding-up petition if the debt is not paid immediately [see page 176] and creates a legal presumption of insolvency.

These legal steps will often follow equally obvious warning signs: you'll no doubt have received final demands for payment, have been refused further supply, or had your account referred to a debt collection agency. The threatening letters are just one step before the strict legal test and it's important to take action at this stage, while there is still time.

'Not yet'

The early signs that I have called 'not yet' are really where you need to review the situation of the business and take remedial action. You have not yet received notice of legal proceedings but you are well on the way there. You find yourself stretching some suppliers' credit terms in order to pay others — and these suppliers may include your landlord or HMRC. You may just delay sending out the cheque for a few days, perhaps making sure it is posted just before a weekend to give you a few more days before it clears. But isn't this normal, doesn't everyone do it? The answer is a matter of scale and duration: if creditors are substantially stretched and it happens every month, it is decidedly not normal. There are three things you can do to assess whether there is a problem:

1. **List all your delayed payments and add up the total.**
2. **Make an estimate of the average delay.**
3. **Check what your minimum bank balance was during these few days of delay.**

The results will give you a good idea of whether you have a problem and how big it is. Let's say you delayed paying £50,000 for a week after the month-end; and suppose you have a bank overdraft facility of £50,000 which was used to the extent of £45,000 during the first few days of the month. That is good, isn't it? You had £5,000 of your bank facility unused. No, it is not good because you used most of the bank facility but did not pay £50,000. That means you are short of the £50,000 you did not pay, less the £5,000 of unused facility — leaving a hole of £45,000 full of debts you could not pay when they fell due.

Maybe you have become so used to delaying payments that it has come to seem normal. It isn't. Most businesses have some variation in their cash flow, either as a result of seasonality or paying rent quarterly. Make sure you do this exercise around the rent quarter day so that you see the worst case.

If this exercise shows that there is a continuing cash shortage, there is one more step to take. Ask yourself:

- **Is the problem getting worse?**
- **Are creditors getting annoyed about the persistent delays?**

If the problem *is* getting worse, you can't just struggle on: a crisis point will come eventually. So it's ok if it's not getting worse? Well... maybe... but, you can pay a week late, every month, for years and then find the suppliers suddenly say 'no more!'. Believe me, I have been there. If you are close to the edge and one supplier who you have been paying, say, £5,000 a month (but a week late) for years suddenly gets awkward or changes their credit controller and the new person says 'no more', where does the extra £5,000 you need come from?

The second point on the list of indicators that show you may have a problem is the forecast. This tells you there will be a future problem that may be days, weeks or months away but it represents a hole that needs some action to close. Just because it is possible to think of many ways of addressing the issue does not remove the problem. Which of these actions will you take and when? In particular, adjusting your forecast assumptions to close the hole, is not (necessarily) a solution. It is too easy. If your first set of assumptions was arrived at with care and consideration but produced a result that you, or someone else, did not like, then adjusting those assumptions threatens to replace a realistic view with wishful thinking — which is dangerous in business.

What about having a balance sheet that shows a deficit — this means your liabilities are bigger than your assets? This is a probable sign that you won't be able to pay your debts at some time in the future but that may not be absolutely certain. You probably need advice. The company may be kept alive by a loan from a director or shareholder. As long as this is not withdrawn, the company is not insolvent, regardless of the balance sheet deficit. Or it may be that the value of some assets in the balance sheet are understated, or there is a reasonable likelihood that a new project will rectify the deficit. Give yourself a moment to think about the opposite problem — suppose the balance sheet looks ok but you know there are some assets there that are not really worth the stated value. This may be stocks that you know you will never sell, or debtors who are never going to pay, or a machine that is actually redundant and worth nothing, or a property that will never find a buyer, or an intangible asset (this may be goodwill arising from an acquisition or be the value of a brand name or a patent etc.). Adjust these values to something you think more realistic: how does the balance sheet look now? If an intangible asset in your balance sheet is what stands between solvency and insolvency, get advice from an accountant.

The fourth indicator of a serious problem — fear of withdrawal of banking facilities — is really just a special case of a forecast assumption that we discussed above, but is so important that it deserves a separate category. Normally any executive of a business that has bank borrowings will, as a matter of course, assume the bank will continue to lend, but what if they don't? It is most likely to prove a problem when the business has or expects cash difficulties or where the balance sheet looks weak. Any of these may prompt a lender to decide the risk is too great and to withdraw facilities. Most companies, from the biggest to the smallest, from the successful to the struggling, will cease to trade if their bankers withdraw facilities. Of course big, successful companies will usually find other bankers or alternative sources of finance in time to prevent insolvency. Smaller companies may find this harder. Of course you can't spend your life worrying about what the bank may or may not do at some point in time. You should reserve your worrying to periods when you know there is a credit crisis affecting banks or if you know that your trading or balance sheet will concern the bank manager.

Should company directors worry about economic conditions or a banking crisis that they can't do anything about? Sure, if this will affect the wellbeing of their business. Credit crises come pretty regularly — maybe every ten or twenty years, certainly once in a working lifetime. It is not as though they are a once-in-a-thousand-year phenomenon. And there are things the individual can do about the potential problem even if not about the economy.

The letter from your accountant

There is another indicator of trouble that I have not included in my list, which is the letter from your external accountant (or, equally, a memo from an internal accountant) that tells you there is a problem. I haven't included it because they, in turn, will have relied upon one of the four indicators I have listed. Nonetheless, this deserves a mention.

The letter from your accountant may follow work on an audit; they may be warning you that they will not be able to give a 'clean' audit opinion or the fact may simply come out of the blue. Any letter of this kind that does not follow a discussion, either in person or over the telephone, is likely to result from someone wanting to 'cover themselves' if things go wrong. They have assessed that the balance of business risk has got worse and could have repercussions for them, so they want something in writing to show they performed their duty and gave due warning.

This is a moment for calm. It may just represent an insurance policy for the writer but it does put the directors in a difficult position. The letter must be read carefully, its implications discussed with the writer and its content must be communicated to the board. The board must discuss the matter and its discussions must be minuted so that, in the event of later liquidation, there is a record that the warning was taken seriously and appropriate action taken. This is a defence against an accusation of wrongful trading. The actions of the directors will depend upon whether the letter warns that the company is insolvent or just that there is a risk it is heading that way. Accepting the message is only one option — the board can decide that it is patently wrong, or it can seek advice from another accountant or from an insolvency practitioner. If the board concludes that it is reasonable to believe that the business can continue as a going concern, their hand is not necessarily forced by the letter. But if that conclusion is *unreasonable*, they do risk legal action for wrongful trading if they continue trading and the business subsequently goes into liquidation.

The audit opinion

An external audit of the financial accounts is no longer required for smaller companies[2] but many still have one, to reassure outside investors, or the bank or even suppliers. Auditors supply a statement for inclusion with the accounts that, amongst other things, gives an opinion that the business is a 'going concern'. Such an opinion can sometimes be qualified. In an extreme case it could say that the going concern status is not appropriate but that rarely happens because the directors would have to call in administrators

2 Turnover less than £6.5m and a balance sheet total less than £3.26m. Companies Act 2006 (Amendment) (Accounts and Reports) Regulations 2008.

before issuing such accounts. Other qualifications may refer to fundamental uncertainty, perhaps arising from inadequate records or to some significant degree of uncertainty or risk. A common comment in the audit opinion of a private company relates to continuing financial support from the bank or from a key investor.

A qualification to the going concern opinion may have no effect if it just draws attention, say, to a company's reliance on an investor continuing their loan. However, a new qualification that indicates some doubt over the going concern status can be a bombshell similar to the accountant's letter discussed above. It would require the directors to think very carefully about prospects for the business and about getting advice. It would also have a big effect on bank lenders and suppliers (or credit insurers) when they read it. Unless the directors believe they can put forward a persuasive case to convince these parties to continue supporting the business, some radical action would be needed.

Common causes of financial distress

So what causes these problems? While there are many detailed possibilities, we can usually group them into just three categories:

- **Overtrading**
- **Long-term weakness**
- **Sudden shock to the system.**

Overtrading

Even profitable and successful companies with a big future may find themselves short of cash as a result of their success. This is called overtrading. It results from the simple idea that a growing business needs to invest in working capital to support that growth. This may be in the form of extra stocks, work in progress or debtors that all grow as sales grow but usually do so before enough profit rolls in to finance them. If your sales are growing and you are making profits *but* are increasingly short of cash, you are probably overtrading. In this situation you only have two choices:

1. **cut back your growth so you can live within your resources;**
2. **raise extra capital or borrowings to finance your growth.**

Actually, there is a third action that is an alternative to limiting your rate of growth. You can raise your prices, perhaps only on these 'extra sales' that you struggle to finance. If you are able to do that, the extra profit will either fund growth or will make the business look more attractive to a bank so that it may be willing to lend more.

No, you say, we can delay a payment here and there and we will get through. Maybe you will but recognise that what you are doing is borrowing more — you are forcing your suppliers to lend you money by delaying your payments to them. And if you are continuing to grow beyond your capacity to generate profits to fund the working capital you need, your problems are likely to get worse.

Long-term weakness

If your business is making losses or only small profits year after year, life will be getting harder. You are probably finding it increasingly hard to find the money to increase wages and the directors' incomes may be eroded year after year. This too is a warning signal. Something really has to be done because the business is getting weaker and weaker. Eventually it will just expire or else a shock will come along that it would once have been able to manage but now can't.

Sudden shock to the system

The best run businesses can suffer sudden shocks. These may have been anticipated risks, such as where you knew you were trading with a price-sensitive customer who might shift the business overseas to a low-wage economy; or they might have been unanticipated — a fire, flood or strike affecting a key customer or supplier. The first task is to recognise that this is a problem. Many directors respond to these 'one-offs' by saying that the underlying business is sound and this is just a blip that they will get over. That may all be true, but in order to get to the long-term you have to survive the short-term. If you refuse to recognise that there really is a problem and don't do something about it, the business may fail.

Disaster recovery

All businesses should prepare for one-off threats by having contingency plans. A small business may have this only in the managing director's head but larger, more complex businesses should have more rigorously prepared plans. It is often said, for example, that a major computer failure is a huge risk factor for a business — many fail in the aftermath — but this is one of the easiest things to prepare for before it happens. There may still be a financial consequence but it need not bring down the company. The same goes for the head office burning down or flooding in the area or a hundred other risks. You don't necessarily need to plan for every individual potential disaster but one head-office relocation plan will address a dozen potential causes. You just need to list what needs to be done, and by whom, who the key contacts or resources are, and what their phone numbers/email addresses are. Oh, and don't keep the list only on a computer at head office, which you won't be able to access if a disaster does present itself.

Do the following simple things:

- **Think about what sort of disasters could strike.**
- **Sketch out a disaster recovery plan.**

Every disaster is different, so no common model will fit every one. But the process for thinking it through is common. We are interested only in significant problems relating to the business, and these fall into categories, such as;

- **Loss of information – for example, computers and accounting information.**
- **Loss of communication – either internally or externally, physically or online.**

- Loss of facilities – manufacturing, head office or storage.
- Loss of key people.
- Loss of logistics – this is the inability to move supplies, people or finished goods.
- Loss of supply or customers.

Solutions to the most likely problems should be sketched out so people would know what to do, but the key issue is to do something in advance for those things that cannot be dealt with after the event. For example:

- Back up computer records, particularly accounts and customer/supplier details off-site, so they can be accessed from anywhere.
- Check your insurance policies, including keyman insurance: are they adequate and do they address the critical risks?
- Keep back-up machines or spare parts on hand where this is not prohibitively expensive.
- If you rely on one critical individual, make sure you have others trained to cover at least part of his or her role.
- Identify an alternative for key functions and contacts, including suppliers, customers, markets, bankers, distribution routes and so on.

Legal disputes

Businesses may get embroiled in legal disputes that can become a threat to the entire viability of the enterprise. If dealing with a big landlord, for example, this can be a huge problem. The landlord can afford to retain expensive lawyers and to draw out the duration of the dispute. This has the effect of increasing your costs, since your lawyers will have to respond to theirs and each letter or phone call costs money. It increases your risk since, if you lose, you become liable for the other side's costs. It increases your problem because delaying a final settlement, in itself, may increase the original loss suffered.

We had a large retail unit on the first floor of an upmarket and successful shopping centre. Unfortunately the landlords sold the scheme and, after six months, the new landlord changed the environment in ways that moved it downmarket, taking out beds with trees and flowers and putting in temporary stalls in the mall. They also took out a lift at our end of the centre. The immediate result was a 25% decline in sales, which cut our profits from the unit by 50%. We protested and threatened legal action but, in view of the financial loss we had already incurred, the costs of funding an accountant's report and expert's report and legal costs were prohibitive. We had a meeting, with lawyers present, and agreed on a follow-up. When the follow-up meeting took place, however, we found the other side behaving as if the first meeting had never happened. With repeated inconclusive meetings our own legal fees would bankrupt us before we reached a settlement. The second critical factor was that the moment we actually issued proceedings we would be liable for their legal costs if we lost. Although our barrister thought our chance of success was 70%, we would have been bankrupted if we lost — so we settled for a fraction of what we thought was right.

Dealing with legal disputes

- Join a trade association that provides legal advice and insurance.
- Check your property and business insurance to see whether you are covered for legal and other professional fees (such as surveyors or valuers).
- Investigate legal dispute finance. This is only available for cases where the finance company believes there is at least a 70% probability of success. It is also usually only available for cases where the sum in dispute is at least £0,5m. The company will fund the legal process in return for a share

of the settlement. It will usually be necessary to use their lawyers and they may require the right to settle on terms they may determine.

- Write letters, send emails and make telephone calls that convince the other side that you will be a major drain on their management time and that you won't go away.
- Look at alternative dispute resolution processes such as arbitration that may be much cheaper than litigation.

What to do
Short-term problems

So we have discussed the four signs that indicate a business may have a solvency problem. We will deal later with the detail of options to pursue. But one more question — is the issue short-term or seasonal, or is it fundamental? If there is a cash problem every year but it just lasts a month, the actions that should be taken may be very different from those addressing a problem that persists month after month and which seems to be getting worse. The seasonal problem, or the one that arises from difficulty financing one piece of business and which will then go away, should probably be addressed by short-term expedients such as getting an extra short-term bank loan or coming to an arrangement with suppliers to cover this short period.

As a retail bookseller we increased our stocks dramatically at Christmas — the main selling season. We might easily have 50% more stock in the shops. However, that would have put enormous pressure on our cash flow, so it was common practice in the trade to get longer credit on this extra stock. Instead of getting 30 or 60 days credit we would get 90 days. This is one reason why the end of March is a common time for retail businesses that are in trouble to call in administrators: the suppliers need paying for Christmas stock at just the time when quarterly rents are due.

Long-term problems

If the problem is fundamental, new strategies are needed and they'll probably be associated with one or more of the following measures:

- **raising more capital;**
- **negotiating larger borrowing facilities;**
- **restructuring.**

You need to think through the underlying causes of the problem and come up with a new strategy before rushing out to apply a bandage to the wound. The sequence of events has to be LOOK—AIM—FIRE and not in any other order. FIRE—AIM—LOOK really doesn't work very well.

Getting advice

If you recognise you may have a financial problem, you will need to get advice. It may feel a little early to be discussing outside advice before you have read the rest of the book (and particularly before the next chapter), but it is useful to have the options in mind as soon as possible.

Many company directors have skills, expertise and experience that lead them to believe they will not gain anything from an outsider. That may be true but remember the old joke that a barrister who represents himself in court has a fool for a client. Having independent, dispassionate advice from someone with a fresh perspective can be immensely helpful, even if they don't know as much about your business as you do. The emotional baggage carried by people who are closely involved in a business can be a hindrance in recognising something that is obvious to an outsider. For example, how many retailers think their shops are at the leading edge of fashion, their staff and the environment welcoming, when an unconnected individual (and the customers who don't visit) will immediately take a different view?

Who do you go to and what sort of advice do you need?

When the wheels come off, most boards of directors will turn to a business adviser, company rescue adviser or their accountant in the first instance. Sometimes one adviser, such as your auditors, may recommend talking to a company rescue specialist. Often the choice is made as a result of personal contacts: just like engaging a plumber or a decorator, you want a personal recommendation from someone you trust, or you will use someone you have used before. That is perfectly natural, but don't choose someone just because you know them in another context. Of course you need to talk to someone you trust, but you also need to talk to someone who will give sound advice in *this particular set of circumstances*; so think first about what advice you need.

The first step is probably getting help in analysing the problem and considering the options. How big is the problem? Is it getting worse? How reliable is the management information? This sort of question requires financial expertise and so the advice sought will probably need to be from someone with an accounting background who can get to grips with the scope of the problem. You will need someone who has some experience of companies in financial distress, even if that is only because they have been through it themselves. This is because they need some awareness of what you are going through, what may happen (such as bailiffs calling), and what range of options is available.

However, the next stage is analysing the causes of the problem and, through that understanding, trying to explore what actions to take. This is a more strategic approach and may need different skills. On the other hand, many business advisers, company rescue specialists and accountants will believe they have these skills too. Check this by discussing options and looking for an open mind and an innovative approach. If the approach offered by a prospective adviser just seems to be a tick-box procession towards insolvency, they may not be the right advisers for this stage.

Often the board of directors will, in reality, be aware of the causes of their problems, and of what they need to do, but have difficulty dealing with their differences of opinion. For example, they may know that they are getting slow or inadequate information from their finance director, or they may recognise the sales director is simply not achieving the sales required, but be unwilling to replace them. The inappropriate or under-performing individual may be a close relative or a friend. In other cases such people may even be performing well but changed circumstances mean the business does not need them or cannot afford them. Tough decisions have to be made.

Justin Cooke faced a stark choice when the dotcom bubble burst. Having spent the previous few years chasing growth rather than profit, the web design entrepreneur had two options: kill off his business or pare it back and try to weather the storm.

He chose the latter even though it meant sacking 75% of his 60 staff, including an old friend who was best man at his wedding. 'I looked at the task ahead of me and decided that I could do it,' Cooke said. 'Even though it would be hard, it would be worth it.'

Fortune Cookie, based in Clerkenwell, on the fringe of the City of London, now turns over £8m and employs 100 people.[3]

In such cases it may be necessary to have an adviser whose skill is to work with people and build confidence whilst steering them towards dealing with the hard choices. In other cases, when the board genuinely has no idea what to do, the requirement may be for a strategist who can put forward a wide range of ideas and suggest options.

It may be at the end of this stage of examining your position and considering alternative options that the adviser will suggest talking to an insolvency practitioner. This is simply an accountant

---

3 Bridge, Rachel. 'How I made it: Justin Cooke, founder of Fortune Cookie', *The Sunday Times*. 9 January 2011.

or lawyer who is authorised by their professional body to act as an administrator, supervisor etc. in insolvency proceedings. Sometimes the original adviser will also be qualified to act and so there is no need to take anyone else on. Turning to an insolvency practitioner does not necessarily mean that the decision has been taken to seek an insolvency solution, but an adviser with this background will be able to provide guidance around the complex legal issues that may equally limit or extend your choices.

There may be an additional need for legal advice because the law in these areas can be complex and relies heavily in the UK on case law that is constantly evolving.

Disagreement among directors

What if the directors of a business disagree? Perhaps some believe the business is insolvent and should stop trading whilst others believe it will recover. There may be a major piece of business in the offing that, if secured, will rescue the company. Some directors think it is just about to be awarded whilst others think that waiting and hoping is too great a risk. The risk is that if a business is not solvent and has no reasonable chance of recovery, continuing to trade may constitute wrongful trading which can open up the individual directors to criminal charges (of fraudulent trading) and to being personally liable for losses incurred.

These disputes fall into different types. The directors may disagree:

- **over whether the business is insolvent or whether it will recover in the normal course of trading;**
- **over what practical business steps to take to save it. This is a dispute about strategy.**

In the first case, the board should seek expert advice and, if they will not, the individual concerned should take personal advice from an insolvency practitioner or from a lawyer who is familiar with insolvency law. Resignation may be an option but may not save the individual from potential liability.

A dissenting director should ensure that meetings are minuted, including a record of their disagreement. If that does not provide enough detail, the dissenting director should also write to fellow directors, perhaps via a memo, recording both the disagreement and the reasons behind it.

The second case is a common management dispute and is discussed below.

A digression about accounts

This is not a book about finance or accounting but it needs a brief digression in to some critical ideas about accounting for the non-financial reader.

Today, double-entry book-keeping is used to manage not just businesses but also charities and government bodies. In fact, it is an immensely powerful technique for managing the financial transactions of any organisation. It works on just a small number of basic principles.

The balance sheet

The balance sheet is a balance of assets and liabilities. Its principle is that the value of any assets that are owned by the entity must be balanced by someone owning — or having a claim on — them. So:

- **fixed assets, stocks, debtors etc. are all assets on one side of the balance sheet;**
- **shareholders' funds, loans, creditors etc. are liabilities on the other side; and**
- **the two sides must add up to the same amount.**

Note a really important point: loans and creditors are a liability of the business. Monies are owed to these people and organisations. That means that they have a claim on the assets of the business to the value of what they are owed. For a company in difficulties, this can result in their total claims being worth as much as, or more than, the total assets of the business. If that is the case then, in order for the two sides of the balance sheet to have the same total, the share due to the owners of the business, or shareholders, must be zero or must have a negative value. For a partnership or sole trader, that would mean that they owe money to the business — which they can be asked to pay in — but a limited liability company is set up so that the shareholders can't lose any more money than that which was paid in for their shares. They cannot be pursued by creditors to make good any shortfall and so that shortfall is a loss to the creditors. The value due to shareholders is called 'shareholders' funds' or 'net worth'. A zero or negative net worth is an indicator that the business may be insolvent.

The balance sheet is a snapshot of a business at a given point in time. We are all familiar with annual balance sheets relating to an arbitrary financial year-end established for the business when it was first set up. But you can draw up a balance sheet at any point in time and most accounting systems have a balance sheet included in the monthly accounts that is used to manage the business.

The balance sheet deals with what can be measured and what is known. It also deals with the past and not the future, so even though a business is just about to win an order that will bring in profits that will repair the shortfall referred to above, nothing of that can be included in the balance sheet.

Double entry

Leading on from the idea of the balance sheet is the idea of double entry. Double entry means that any change in an asset or liability that is recorded on one side of the accounts has to be matched by an entry of the same size on the other side of the accounts, so that an increase in assets automatically means there is an increase in liabilities of exactly the same value — or a decrease in a different asset. Without this rule, the balance sheet would not balance. Remember here that the value due to shareholders is actually termed a 'liability' because it describes value that is due from the business to someone outside the business — the shareholders.

This leads to the slightly counter-intuitive idea that profit, which is the excess of sales revenues over costs, goes on the 'liabilities' side of the balance sheet. This is because the profit is due to the shareholders. Another way of looking at it, for a simple cash sale, is that the cash coming in from the sale is an increase in the assets of the business; it is matched, in part, by a decrease in another asset, stock which is on the same side of the balance sheet. The remaining part of the balance is profit from the sale, which shows up on the other side of the balance sheet. For example;

ASSETS		LIABILITIES	
Increased cash	10	Increased profit	2
Decreased stock	8		

Matching

Which brings us to the third idea, which is that the accounts match transactions to the period in which they occur. So if the business sells something in period 1, its stocks show a matching reduction in that period and the profit is recorded in that period even though the cash is not paid by the customer until period 2. In the meantime, the amount due is shown as a debtor to the business.

Failure of financial reporting systems

One of the common features of financial distress is that financial control is weak. The directors and managers of a business frequently don't have full, up-to-date and accurate information: they are flying blind. Why is this? One reason is that poor accounting systems themselves lead to problems. If, as a decision maker, you are unaware that there is a problem, then you are likely to invest money that should be conserved, and you won't realise your stock levels are too high, or that your debtors are not paying on time or that creditors are pressing.

Of course, some of these issues should be obvious without accounting information. Walking around the business premises should reveal when stock levels are too high. However, there may always be reasons why such things are not noticed but the financial numbers should give early warning.

Another reason is that as difficulties mount so the individuals who are meant to be measuring and reporting divert their energies to other matters. They get involved in too many 'fire-fighting' issues and argue that the urgent drives out the important. They also become stressed and perform less well (see next chapter).

The third possibility is that the financial function simply fails. Individuals perform inadequately and either do not produce accurate, timely and meaningful information or fail to analyse it to show an emerging problem.

There is also a final cause that is often overlooked. It is your fault. What I mean is that the non-financial directors put pressure on the finance staff. In some cases this is just the chief executive insisting 'The profit margin must be better than that', which pushes the accountant to make the optimistic assumptions that will show the desired result on paper. Perhaps the chief executive does not want the bank, or the head office, or investors, or credit reference agencies to know that trading is poor. Maybe they want to resolve issues on their own. So pressure is brought to make optimistic assumptions or even to hide things.

I was appointed as acting finance director for a large engineering subsidiary of the company I worked for, after the previous finance director was removed for dishonesty. The business made enormous machine tools, and I soon noticed that large sums of development expenditure had been applied to a particular development project. A few enquiries rapidly revealed that what had been happening was that, in order to improve reported results, the finance director — probably in collusion with the previous managing director — had been moving all sorts of spending to the account of this machine. Presumably he hoped that business would pick up and it could be reallocated at some time, or maybe he hoped the machine would actually be sold. Since the machine in question would probably never be sold he was actually parking business losses in a holding account and hoping for the best.

The lesson of this story is not just to keep an eye out for dishonesty but, more importantly, to be aware of the dangers of putting pressure on the finance function to produce results that the business itself can't achieve.

Critical financial indicators

There are many financial measures that can be used to give warning of problems or can help to analyse causes and solutions. These may be ratios or absolute numbers and it is usually their trend that is important. Look at these trends over months and years. What is important will vary by industry but some things are universal.

Key financial indicators should include:

- **Sales levels compared with budget.**
- **Order book.**
- **Stock levels (divided into raw materials, work-in-progress and finished goods).**
- **Stocks as a percentage of sales.**
- **Aged stocks.**
- **Debtors (also compared as a percentage of sales).**
- **Aged debtors.**
- **Creditors (as a percentage of purchases).**
- **Aged creditors.**
- **Labour costs as a percentage of sales.**
- **Gross and net profit (as a percentage of sales).**

Cash generation is important: a business that seems profitable but never seems to produce any cash may be one you don't want to be involved with. However, simple measures can oversimplify; Amazon, for example, took eight years before it reached profitability, requiring huge amounts of continuing investment. Eventually, of course, it became highly profitable.

Frequently used ratios include:

- **Current ratio — current assets divided by current liabilities.**
- **Acid test — current assets (less stocks) divided by current liabilities.**

These two indicate how liquid the business is — how easily and quickly it can produce cash. But financial analysis is not necessarily straightforward. A business that has lots of slow-moving stock may have an apparently good current ratio. Another that is squeezing its creditors will have more cash and therefore a better acid test ratio, but this will not be a sign of good financial health. Any ratios therefore need to be read in conjunction with others — so poor stockturn or bad average stock age will reveal that the good current ratio is misleading. The extending trend of creditor days will indicate that a sound acid test is likewise misleading.

CHAPTER 2
DEALING WITH THE STRESS OF FINANCIAL DISTRESS

When a company is in financial distress, there are usually human causes and human consequences. These are as varied as the businesses and people who suffer them, but tend to fall within broad categories which enables them to be recognised and understood. And the only way of avoiding or dealing with them is to recognise them. Once you've done that, you can work out how to tackle them.

Human causes
Personal relationships

It is common for the performance of a business to be damaged by key people simply not getting on. You can't change people's personalities, but you can change their behaviours and you can change the processes an organisation uses to operate. So once the problem is recognised and accepted, there may be steps that can reduce (if not eliminate) the effects of strain.

- **Reach an accommodation. Individuals do not need to like each other to work together effectively. If they can recognise the damage their clashes are having, however, there's a chance they will agree to resolve them in less damaging ways. They may refer them to someone else to mediate or adjudicate; or they may deal with them in a board meeting rather than yelling at each other in the office.**

- **Separate the individuals.** If people don't get on, perhaps their roles can be reorganised so they don't have much personal interaction.
- **Use intermediaries.** Unfortunately it is common for problems between departmental heads to poison the relationships of subordinates too but nonetheless it may help to delegate contact between departments.
- **Terminate employment.** This is a drastic course of action but may be better than living with constant strife.

Disagreements over strategy

Disagreement over strategy is often a euphemism for personal clashes. If individuals have conflicting interpretations of agreed strategy or, more straightforwardly, don't agree the strategy

As a director of a retail business I was taking prime responsibility for an Internet activity we had developed. I saw this as critical to our survival because the performance of the shops was deteriorating. I believed we had no choice but to make this part of the business work. Unfortunately my co-directors were less convinced of its viability and importance, which caused constant clashes over how I allocated my time.

In the final analysis, if you don't agree with the consensus you have three practical choices; persuade the others, compromise or leave. Of course, each company has a different dynamic that governs how it takes decisions. In some, the managing director dominates and can enforce a decision even if there is a majority of the board who oppose it. In such companies, only a vote to remove the individual from their post will change the decision. In other organisations, the view of the consensus does predominate. In yet others, individual directors may ignore board decisions and follow their own conflicting policies, often disguising what they are doing.

itself, they must reach an agreement or someone must step in and force a unity of direction.

Rivalry

Straightforward personal rivalry can be highly motivating but can also, when taken too far, be highly damaging.

XYZ was a manufacturing business. Its purchasing department had to place orders four months before stock was needed and relied upon the sales department for sales forecasts which would indicate how much would be manufactured and therefore what components would be required. However, these forecasts looked three months ahead. The obvious thing was for the sales department to produce four month forecasts but, because of rivalries, this never happened and the business suffered stock shortages or excess. This was a case for the Managing Director to take matters in hand and lay down the law.

Underperformance

Dealing with underperforming staff isn't easy. The individuals may be long-standing personal friends or even relatives. Many family businesses will end up carrying sons or daughters, sisters or brothers, even though it is clear that they are not performing their roles effectively. Sometimes this can be addressed in the short term by allocating another employee to shadow the role that isn't being performed, but the problem will have to be tackled more appropriately at some stage. When someone does a bad job, there are three sets of effects: the direct damage due to the poor performance; the strain on others who have to cover; and lower morale all round.

Performance issues should be dealt with through an appraisal system which brings individuals to a clear understanding of business and personal goals and what they need to do to improve their performance.

Human consequences

Many of the consequences of stress cause further deterioration of the financial position, increase the stress and create, in their turn, further consequences.

Poor or postponed decision-making

Under stress, people may panic and take snap decisions that are not fully considered and may make things worse. Alternatively, frozen by uncertainty, the urgent decision is not made and things get worse.

Avoidance behaviour

It is quite common for stressed executives to actively avoid taking unavoidable decisions. An executive seems to be functioning normally until the business reaches a crisis that colleagues were unaware was approaching. The individual is removed from office and it is discovered that their desk drawer is full of unopened bills, final demands and court documents. This is no apocryphal story: it happens ever day. The individual can see no solution to the problem and so they avoid it for as long as possible, even though they know that a crisis will inevitably result eventually.

Poor communication

As colleagues recognise they have problems, they may seek to talk about them, but they may equally shut themselves in their departmental responsibilities and stop communicating. This behaviour may arise from deteriorating relationships (see below) or it may result from the kind of avoidance behaviour discussed above. To make matters worse, failure to communicate feeds resentment, which in turn contributes to fraught relationships. The only way of finding a solution to most problems is through open communication, which means not just answering questions but also volunteering information and actively encouraging responses and ideas.

Rocky relationships

It's common for colleagues to turn on each other in difficult times rather than trying to work together to find a way out. Now this is not totally irrational. If you believe that colleague X has got you into a mess, either as a result of not doing their job well or through bad decisions, it may be sensible to try to exclude them from further decisions. In this way, you avoid the results of further ineptitude. The problems with this, however, are:

- **energy is diverted to infighting rather than directed at resolving the problem;**
- **even if everyone is addressing the problem, you may be pulling in different directions;**
- **the person you are no longer co-operating with, even if they really are the cause of the problem, may hold the key to getting out of it.**

It is not certain but it is at least possible that communicating and co-operating as a team may be the only way to avoid catastrophe. At least give it a try.

CHAPTER 3
AVOIDING INSOLVENCY

Once you recognise that your business has financial problems — and just doing that is a big step — you must then identify whether it can be turned around before you can identify what to do. This is easier said than done. And if anyone, at this stage says 'failure is not an option', please take them out and shoot them. Confidence is a great virtue and when allied with real determination can be a powerful force to create a successful business. However, it is also vital to come to terms with reality and not to continue banging your head against a brick wall. Failure is *always* an option, unfortunately. There are situations that cannot be salvaged. Going away and starting another business or changing career may be sensible options and lead to future success. Refusing to accept reality can leave you older (too old to find alternative employment) and poorer (having wasted resources that would have started a new business).

The steps to take are:

- **recognise the existence of a problem;**
- **analyse its causes;**
- **review whether these can be addressed, leading to a solution;**
- **examine possible options;**
- **compare these options with personal goals before taking action.**

As directors of a small retail chain, we recognised that we faced serious structural changes in our market: supermarkets and online sellers posed serious and growing price competition for our highest volume products — whilst there was no easing of cost pressures to compensate. Could we overcome this squeeze? We clearly could not compete head-on against entities that were orders of magnitude bigger than us, so were there market niches available to us or other products?

We decided that it was still possible to return to profitable growth if we could establish our own online business or if we could make a radical change to our cost base by shrinking our head office. As a first stage we began to sell slower-moving products from our stores through online intermediaries, also developing a business that bought end-of-line stock in bulk at discounted prices to sell online.

Do not make a decision to struggle on without believing there is a plausible strategy that stands a reasonable chance of achieving a turnaround.

Years of working hard but failing to halt gradually declining sales and profitability are demoralising and a waste of your time. Go and do something else because it will become gradually harder to change direction with every passing year.

So you have thought about this and believe there is a viable strategy; you still have to get over the short-term financial problems you have recognised in order to get to the long-term strategy.

A digression: the immediate and urgent

If you have one or more county court judgements against you or bailiffs have called or you have received a statutory demand there are some immediate things to do. You *must* have recognised there is a problem and are working through the steps listed above but you need to get to tomorrow. First — get advice, and that is dealt with below. Second, there is always a good chance that there is a way out of the financial crisis but the potentially business closing legal threat *must* be dealt with before options can be examined. Always consider that it may be possible to negotiate with your creditor. They want to be paid — putting your company into liquidation may not achieve that. If you are at this point you probably can't find the money to just pay them and get them off your back. You can try other routes such as:

- **ask them to delay their legal process for a few days while you try to find a longer-term solution;**
- **agree a payment schedule of, at least, some of the debt;**
- **offer to return some of the stock they have supplied to you;**
- **offer some form of security;**
- **involve them in the solution — show them your business recovery plan and persuade them that there will be a real reward if they support you just now.**

Be creative and find just a little space to find a solution.

What are the options?

Business is not that complicated; there are only three things you can do (everything else is just detail):

- **increase your revenues;**
- **cut your costs;**
- **raise extra finance.**

Increase revenues

You have probably already thought about ways to increase your revenues. Selling more of your products or services is a key part of your day-to-day business and presumably you would have already increased your prices if that were possible. Even at this stage, however, it is worth thinking through these things once again, particularly because you may now be prepared to do something more drastic than you considered before. For example, perhaps:

- one part of your product range is more profitable than the rest and could be concentrated on, perhaps even at the expense of other parts;
- cutting prices might increase sales more than it cuts your profit margin;
- you could offer your salespeople a higher commission incentive;
- there is a new channel to market you have not tried before?

But be careful not to increase your selling costs *before* you achieve extra sales: you already have one pressing financial challenge and don't want to add to the problem.

However... suppose you can think of a way of increasing revenue but it's a way which requires an extra investment. This can be a really tough choice. Is it a gamble that risks pouring good money after bad? You'll need to assess:

- the investment required;
- the reward it will produce;
- the probability of success;
- the risks that would lead to failure;
- your appetite for risk.

Cut costs

When you look at costs, start with the big numbers — they'll be where you can make big savings. Look again at property rents: can you move premises or negotiate with landlords? Can you renegotiate equipment rentals?

I had just taken on a part-time role as Director of IT for a subsidiary company of the group where I was Director of Business Development. We were anxious to cut the very high costs of our computing and a newspaper article had brought to my attention that the leasing deal provided by our main supplier was actually quite an expensive option. I ran the numbers and confirmed that this was true, but we were tied in to a long-term contract so I couldn't do anything about it. Wrong. There is always something you can do. I demanded a meeting with our supplier's sales manager and the head of the business division he represented. I screamed and shouted and banged the table and accused them of exploitation and threatened to walk away from the contracts and see them in court. This particular approach will not always work but in the light of the newspaper article that alerted me to the issue it was worth a try. And it did work. I cut our costs by £150,000 a year.

By this stage, you have probably gone through your costs time and time again and cut them as much as you can. Beyond that, would restructuring the business make a really significant difference? Consider:

- **stopping some areas of activity entirely (this would allow you to sell off all the stock and machinery associated with it, releasing cash for the rest of the business. Cutting an activity may also reduce overheads;**
- **changing the way you do something, like buying in a component or contracting out the manufacturing or the entire sales function;**
- **checking whether a big supplier will supply you on a consignment basis, billing you only when you sell the goods;**
- **cutting the level of stock you hold by getting the supplier to hold some for you;**
- **asking customers to pay a deposit with their order or to pay progress payments as their order is manufactured.**

Raise extra finance

This absolutely depends upon your belief that there is a viable business: raising extra finance is rarely a solution in its own right but it can be a key solution if the business is under-capitalised.

To give you time for your survival strategy to give results or to finance the extra cost of the new strategy, there are many things that can be done, such as:

- **raising extra investment from new or existing shareholders;**
- **borrowing more from your bank or finance company;**
- **persuading suppliers to invest or to give you longer credit;**
- **persuading customers to invest in the business;**
- **using debt factoring;**
- **selling assets.**

A company that is profitable but simply does not have enough working capital will, of course, go to their bank for help. However, it is often the case that they can't offer sufficient security. One possible solution is the Enterprise Finance Guarantee Scheme, which is a government-backed loan scheme that guarantees 75% of the loan for an extra fee (an additional 2%). It still does not ensure that a bank will advance a loan but it does improve the chances.

This scheme is available for companies with up to £25m turnover and for amounts between £1,000 and £1m. Lists of qualifying industries and banks that operate the scheme are on the Department for Business, Innovation and Skills (BIS) website. Application is made to the bank which will then apply for the guarantee to the BIS (http://www.bis.gov.uk/policies/enterprise-and-business-support/access-to-finance/enterprise-finance-guarantee). The bank may still seek additional personal guarantees from directors but, unlike normal commercial loans, may not take a charge over a principle private residence.

If the shortage of working capital relates to export business it may be possible to raise extra loans to finance it with the assistance of the Export Credits Guarantee Department that provides insurance and guarantees to commercial banks to support export business (http://www.ecgd.gov.uk).

One way of raising finance is to reduce working capital, which has exactly the same effect as borrowing money from the bank but with the bonus of you not paying any interest! There are several ways to do this.

Reduce stocks
- **Sell slower moving stocks at a large discount to shift them.**
- **Cut the product range, reducing work-in-progress.**
- **Supply only to order.**
- **Get suppliers to hold stock for quick delivery to you.**
- **Sub-contract so other people hold stocks not you.**

Reduce debtors
- **Ask for a deposit with each order.**
- **Reduce payment terms, say from 60 to 30 days.**
- **Increase prices but then offer the money back as a fast payment discount.**
- **Make sure your debtors are chased the moment an account becomes due — or even before.**

Increase creditors
- **Be firm with suppliers who date their invoices before the month-end but despatch them only after it has passed.**
- **Apply for longer credit terms.**
- **Simply take a few days extra credit.**

This last point is contentious because those suppliers may not be happy that you are taking more credit and they may react in ways that will harm your business. This is, then, as you'd expect, not a long-term solution. Nonetheless, if you have a problem, it is always worth revisiting this point: it may buy extra time to find another solution and, sometimes, some suppliers don't seem to notice even when others would react badly.

Management issues

Avoiding bankruptcy may demand skills you don't have available. Managing a crisis effectively can demand skills that are different from those required to set up a business or maintain a successful one. Getting through tough times may call for a particular analytical ability, financial training, the willingness to knock heads together or take unpopular decisions. Alternatively the need may be for a particular skill just for a few months. You have decided what needs doing but that includes (for example) a new website, a new marketing strategy or a new product and you need help to set these up.

Money is short, what do you do? Despite the financial strain, money must be spent to save the day. Your options include:

- **temporary support from your accountants;**
- **turnaround specialists;**
- **interim management;**
- **outside consultants.**

A firm's regular accountants can often provide extra support to install new control systems or to provide analytical support. They can often second staff for a period, perhaps part-time. This may be a much cheaper option than bringing in consultants.

Turnaround specialists tend to be more used to raising funds, organising restructuring or dealing with near-terminal crises. They are less used to the more mundane day-to-day management.

Interim managers are people who work as part of the business but for periods of a few months to a year or so. They provide the extra resource that is required, for as long as it is needed. They can provide any sort of skill from technical to general management. Many recruitment firms as well as specialist agencies will provide interim managers.

Whether it be in specialist areas such as human resources or more multi-disciplinary areas such as strategy development, there are many firms that offer consultancy services. They can provide the specialist expertise that a company cannot afford in-house, the cross-fertilisation of ideas across many businesses and an external, dispassionate viewpoint. The individuals or teams involved do what it says on the tin, they consult, they do not manage or make decisions. A big caveat in using consultancy services is that you, the client, must avoid using them just to add credibility to what you wanted to do anyway. Used in that way the consultant does not provide new ideas but may reinforce the limited thinking that got you into this fix in the first place.

The business plan

A business plan is vital to fight off insolvency. It performs three distinct functions:

- **It plans what to do.**
- **It persuades people to lend or invest money.**
- **It persuades business partners to deal with you.**

Plans what to do

Don't underestimate the value of a plan in guiding your own actions. The very act of going through the discipline of writing a plan can help you clarify your thoughts and identify any flaws in what you propose. After writing a plan try to get someone, whose business acumen you respect, to read it and give you feedback. Do not seek out someone who will tell you it is marvellous even if it isn't.

Persuades financiers and investors

Whether you want the bank to continue to lend or you want new money from a bank or investor to see through your proposals, the written explanation is vital.

Persuades business partners

Key suppliers and customers get, understandably, nervous when you are going through a financial crisis. You need them to continue and the business plan is one of the crucial instruments in reassuring them and persuading them. That supposes, of course, that it does portray a credible and persuasive picture.

How is this plan different from any other plan?

I have written books on how to write a business plan and how to make them more effective. This is not the place to repeat that advice but there are some points that stand out as different for businesses suffering financial distress. In particular you need to explain:

- **what went wrong;**
- **what the solution is;**
- **how you propose to implement it;**
- **what the outcome will be;**
- **what the risks are;**
- **why the investor/financier/business partner should back you.**

The heart of this is a story, starting with what went wrong, moving on to what you intend to do about it and finishing with a happy ending — the payoff. You must acknowledge mistakes and show you understand them. You must persuade the reader that you have the will and the ability to turn things around. The management team is critical to this. People back management and not just figures on a sheet of paper. If changes in personnel, reporting lines, or roles are necessary, say so. Be honest about what it will cost and show a willingness to make sacrifices to contribute to this cost. You may be telling your supplier that they will lose part of the debt you owe them but, if that is the case, balance this with benefits — maybe you will be a reliable customer in the future; maybe you can offer them extra payments in compensation when things recover.

Put forward a series of forecasts — both profit and cash forecasts, and probably a balance sheet forecast as well — to show that it all hangs together and the figures reconcile. These must be realistic and conservative. Profits usually take longer to appear than people think but costs almost always arrive early.

Do not show the famous dog-leg graph of profitability — that is one where profits have declined for a period and then suddenly turn upwards, high into the air. It is better to show a realistic improvement, even if it is slow and modest, rather than a dramatic one that nobody believes.

Be open and honest about risks. Every plan of action carries risks. The key approach is to declare them and, at the same time, to explain what you will do if things do go wrong.

Finish by making two things clear to your audience:

- **what it is you are asking them to do;**
- **what their reward will be.**

You may be asking for investment or to write off part of a debt or for time to pay, time to deliver or just to continue trading on the same terms as before. Whatever it is, make it clear and ask for what you need. Don't ask for too little, because there may not be a second chance to do this.

Make it equally clear what the financial return will be to the financier or investor, the good profitability and low risk of your future business to the supplier, and the reliable deliveries you will make to your customer.

And when you present your plan and discuss it, if the investor, the bank or the creditor asks for too much, tell them. If there is not enough in the final deal to motivate you to work incredibly hard to make it succeed, that's no good for anybody. The deal has to be fair to everyone or it will fail for everyone.

CHAPTER 4
PRACTICAL PROBLEMS

The last chapter dealt with general steps a business can take to stave off bankruptcy, but there are still many day-to-day problems to address even if you have addressed the big ones. And these smaller issues can still have the potential to bring an entire business to a halt.

Cessation of service and supply

The most common problem facing a business that has financial difficulties is that one or more suppliers put you on stop: in short, they won't send you any more goods unless you pay what you owe. Actually there is some good news — they are willing to continue supplying you *as long as* you pay what is overdue. Several points here:

- **How important is this supplier? Can you trade without their product or service? Can you get the same product or an alternative from someone else?**
- **Make sure they are willing to continue to supply you *on the same terms as before*. If they want you to pay up in full but still intend not to supply any more then you may feel they are a somewhat lower priority to pay!**
- **I highlighted 'on the same terms as before'. If the price or the credit terms are worse than before then that could make your problems worse.**

• **Companies assign a credit period — say 30 days after the month-end when they deliver — and if you pay late, will stop supplies. However, have you made sure they won't give you 60 days? If your purchases are likely to grow, or if you find their other customers are allowed longer to pay, then this deadline might be moveable. It's always worth asking.**

Make sure you have a reasonable relationship with the credit controller at major suppliers. They might still get angry with you or be instructed by their bosses to be tougher but explaining to them about your short-term problems may persuade them to give you a few days extra time to pay. For a critical supplier you may need to meet a more senior credit controller, or the finance director, in order to negotiate a one-off agreement to have more time to pay, or to reach a continuing agreement. If this is necessary you need to take along financial forecasts to the meeting that show your company is getting back on track and will be able to pay on-time in future. You will also need to explain why you got into this problem and what you are doing about it. Remember that if you are a big customer, it is in the supplier's interests to support you, as long as they don't feel they are throwing good money after bad. If they feel your business is not viable, it makes no sense for them to allow you to build up your debt further — it is better for them to take the hit now.

This highlights a common business dilemma. Do you tell your key supplier(s) that you have financial difficulties, and if so, when? On the one hand, if you tell them in good time they may co-operate with you and help you through your difficulty. On the other hand, they may respond by instantly cutting off supplies and taking legal action to recover their debt. And equally bad, they may tell everyone else in the market about your problem. There is no simple answer to this dilemma — every case is different — but the critical issues to think about are:

• **Can you make a persuasive case that your business will get through this problem and prosper?**

- **As a customer, are you important to the supplier(s)?**
- **Do you have a good relationship with the supplier(s) at a senior level?**
- **Does your supplier use credit insurance?**

If the supplier is convinced that your problem is short-term, will be resolved, and that you will continue to be an important contributor to their business then they will probably be helpful. This will be reinforced if you are important to the supplier's business. Imagine an extreme case — let's suppose you account for 30% of their business — they may feel they have little choice but to support you. How long you have been trading together and whether you have abused their trust before are important considerations. If you have been continually paying them late for the past year, they are likely to be less sympathetic and less helpful. And who your relationship is with is important. Getting on really well with your supplier's sales team may be good but when it comes to extending your credit, it's not the sales team that matters: it is the finance function that matters, and possibly not the credit controller, but the financial controller or finance director. For this, you need a good relationship at a senior level.

Talk to the most senior person you can. Explain your problem and recovery plan and ask for a face-to-face meeting. Once there, present a business plan that explains your proposal and why they should back you.

See page 145 for an example of problems with a supplier who uses credit insurance. Credit insurers tend to be less sympathetic and will be swayed by your credit history and the security promised by your balance sheet. If they refuse to cover your debts, the supplier needs to decide whether to take the risk themselves. It may still be possible to persuade the supplier to do this.

Dealing with tax authorities

Tax authorities are a special kind of supplier. They supply services like roads and hospitals and require paying. They tend to get cross if you persistently pay them even a few days late and may take tough action quite quickly. In other circumstances it is possible to run up quite large overdue sums but tax authorities are unpredictable — you never know how they will act. As a result, it is not a particularly good idea to force them to finance any but short-term and one-off cash flow problems.

Local authorities collect business rates in the UK and many companies will pay them in ten instalments during the year. The authorities may not respond to a few late payments but if late payments become extended and persistent, they will usually send a warning letter threatening to demand immediate payment of the entire outstanding balance. If this does not lead to an improvement then they will carry out their threat and send a letter demanding payment in full within seven days. Local authorities can be quite quick to send in bailiffs beyond this point to seize goods to pay off the debt owed to them. They will seldom send another warning because they do not want the business to remove items from the premises. For a business that has problems, local authorities will often agree a schedule of repayments to clear an outstanding balance. It is important, therefore, to contact them as soon as a demand letter is received. If, say, a three month backlog has built up then they may agree for it to be repaid over several months — on top of a resumption of normal payments.

Companies in the UK collect taxes (PAYE and Employees National Insurance) as deductions from employees' monthly pay and then pay it to Her Majesty's Revenue and Customs (HMRC) by the nineteenth day of the following month together with Employers National Insurance. As with local authorities, they may act firmly on persistent late payment and may also use bailiffs. Before this stage they will often send someone from the local tax office to collect a cheque. VAT collection is much the same. The HMRC website (http://www.hmrc.gov.uk) says:

• **You will not be charged a penalty if only one PAYE amount is late in a tax year — unless that payment is over six months late.**

- **The amount of the penalty will depend on how much is late and how many times your payments are late in a tax year. So if you pay part of what is due on time then any penalty will only be charged on the part that is late.**

The penalties build up depending upon how frequently payment is late — reaching 4% if 11 or 12 are late in a year. There is also a 5% penalty if you are more than six months late, rising to 10% after 12 months. These penalties cannot be offset as a business expense against future tax bills.

If you discover an error after the year-end, report it and pay the outstanding amount, you may still be liable to a penalty for late payment.

Of course, desperate company directors may sometimes under-declare these periodic tax payments, with the intention of declaring an error and paying the full amount later. This may help a business to get through a short-term crisis but it is unlawful and carries some risks. The amounts of money that can be raised in this 'forced loan' from the government may be relatively small and there is a possibility of attracting penalties when it is discovered. This is particularly the case if discovery follows a tax inspection rather than the situation being reported by the company itself. If the amounts of money involved are larger, and it can be shown to have been a deliberate under-declaration, there is a risk of prosecution for fraud. In extreme cases, where a company goes into insolvent liquidation and is found to owe PAYE, NI or VAT beyond just the 'current period', its directors may be personally liable for the deficit and there may be action to disqualify them from being company directors in future.

HMRC time to pay deals

HMRC is often prepared to agree Time to Pay (TTP) arrangements that allow 'viable customers' who cannot pay on the due date to pay by regular monthly payments or at a later date. This is managed through the Business Payment Support Scheme (BPSS). By a 'viable customer', they mean one that will be able to pay if there is a short deferral. HMRC is not a bank and the payment proposals must be the best that the taxpayer can afford — there is no allowance for funds made available through a TTP to be used for investment in new projects.

There are some important points to bear in mind here. These arrangements are typically for a few months although they can be longer: TTPs that last for more than a year are, however, exceptional. The amount of tax due will never be reduced through a TTP arrangement. If any repayments of tax become due during the TTP period, HMRC will offset these against the debt; and a TTP includes payment of interest for taxes received after the due date.

HMRC is bound by TTP agreements that it enters into but may withdraw if:

- **new facts come to light;**
- **information turns out to have been misleading or incorrect;**
- **a payment is missed;**
- **it becomes clear that immediate action is required to protect the total tax due.**

Although time to pay deals can be very helpful, their availability does depend upon HMRC's willingness to be helpful. At the time of writing, HMRC is reported to be going through a period of being tough and focusing on getting monies in rather than deferring collection. The number of approved deals halved between 2009 and 2010. HMRC are therefore asking searching questions and will not offer deals if they think either that the company will not be able to pay in future, or, that it can pay now if squeezed hard. They expect all sources of finance to have been exhausted and, it is reported, even expect company credit cards to have been used, despite the high rates of interest charged. Around 6% of applications for TTP were rejected in 2010.

Dealing with landlords

Commercial landlords are different from other creditors. On top of the rights that all creditors have to send in bailiffs, property leases generally give them two particular rights, if the tenant is in breach of their obligations. Only one of these may be enforced for the same debt:

- **forfeiture**
- **distraint.**

Forfeiture
The lease can be forfeited in either of two ways, by application to the courts or, far cheaper for the landlord, by peaceful re-entry. They just enter the premises and change the locks.

Distraint
A popular tool for landlords (or bailiffs for the Crown) where rent or other payments are not made, distraint means that an agent of the landlord can effect entry to remove goods or assets for sale to pay for the debt due. He/she does not need to wait for a long period for this to happen. In theory, one week after a rent payment is due, they can distrain. Nor is a court judgement necessary. The landlord can send bailiffs in to seize goods to be sold to cover outstanding rent and this does not require an application to the courts.

If a landlord takes or threatens either of these actions to recover rent or service charges in arrears, the tenant should take legal advice because the precise terms of the lease are important. However, negotiation is also important here. The landlord's objective is to be paid and to be paid on time: it is generally not to evict tenants nor to make their situation worse by seizing their stock in trade. Re-letting the property leads to a period with no rent as well as incurring expense (such as agents fees and business rates — whereas in the past empty properties attracted a reduced level of rates, this arrangement only extends for six months now) and aggravation and usually only rises up the landlord's agenda when the tenant is commonly in default and the landlord fears they may become insolvent.

There is, therefore, scope to negotiate. The tenant's strength in such discussions depends upon the current state and prospects for the property market, the ease of letting the particular premises and the particular needs of the landlord. For example, large property companies value their properties on a multiple of rents, so they will be reluctant to agree a reduced rent because that will affect the value in their balance sheet. That does not mean, however, that it is not worth a try. There are several alternatives. Issues that can be negotiated include:

- **payment of rent arrears on an agreed schedule (usually with an undertaking to pay future rents on time);**
- **payment of rent monthly or even weekly (commercial rents are usually paid quarterly in advance);**
- **agreement of a reduced rent (this can be a temporary or permanent reduction or one that is compensated by higher future rents);**
- **agreement to surrender part of the premises occupied;**
- **agreement to sub-let or let 'on licence' to a third party a part of the premises occupied.**

It should be noted that many property leases to smaller businesses will also be accompanied by guarantees from directors. But if there are not any guarantees then a tenant can wind up their company and walk away from the lease [see Administration, Chapter 6].

Dealing with banks

All businesses use banks even if it is for nothing more than receiving and paying out money. Some businesses operate with a continual surplus of funds but most have some sort of borrowing, even if it is only for a seasonal or occasional overdraft. Most businesses cannot continue trading without the support of their bank.

A well-run business will keep in regular touch with its bank manager, will supply regular management accounts and submit year-end accounts promptly. There will be no surprises — banks don't like surprises. The overdraft will never be exceeded and, if it is, one of the directors will have telephoned in advance and explained the short-term issue that will cause this and will have arranged for a temporary excess to be applied.

However, sometimes company directors will face the same dilemma with their bank, as described above, with suppliers. If you tell the bank you have a problem, will they support you or push you over the edge?

What warning signs does your bank look for?

- **Annual accounts — trading losses or balance sheet deficit.**
- **Poor security for overdraft.**
- **Overdraft always close to its limit and sometimes exceeding its limit.**
- **Poor management information, supplied late or not at all.**
- **Delayed filing of annual accounts.**
- **Lack of forecasts or wild inaccuracy.**
- **Lack of commitment from directors.**
- **Lack of co-operation — unwillingness to meet the bank manager or supply information.**
- **Downturn in the particular market a company trades in.**

If annual accounts show continuing losses or very low profitability, a bank manager will be concerned about the viability of a business. They will look at the balance sheet to check what security they have for their loan or overdraft facility and they may seek additional security in the form of personal guarantees.

An apparently strong balance sheet may not be enough to dissuade a bank from seeking personal guarantees. The bank is aware that the balance sheet is prepared on a going concern basis and that, in the case of an insolvency, asset values can fall dramatically.

Evaporating value

A company balance sheet can be produced on a 'going concern' basis or on a 'break-up' basis. These are very different things. If a company ceases to trade and the bank switches to looking at a company in terms of break-up basis, its:

- **Stocks of finished goods** may be worth much less than before, because it can take time to sell them and in a forced sale buyers will pay less. Typically they will realise between 10 and 30% of book value. There may be slow moving stock that would sell through in time but is practically worthless in a quick sale.
- **Work-in-progress** may be valueless unless it is finished.
- **Raw material stocks** will halve in value when you try to sell them back to the supplier. This is partly because you are a forced seller and people take advantage but also because transportation and restocking takes time and effort; also because there may be some damages in transit.
- **Fixed assets** such as plant and machinery will also be worth much less than book value. You may find that nobody is in the market at present for a particular piece of machinery, except at a very low price.
- **Property** is often worth less than the going concern balance sheet figure, particularly if it is held on a lease. If you lease or rent the property, there is a risk that the landlord may repossess it if the company becomes insolvent. Most leases contain a clause that appears to give the landlord the right to repossess property if the tenant becomes insolvent or makes a formal arrangement with creditors. Even if this can be prevented it may prove difficult to get anyone else to take over the property within a short period. And even if someone else does want the property they may not want the lighting, air conditioning or shelving that you put in at great expense and which is in the balance sheet.

The property crunch

You may find yourself looking to shed property during a downturn. The bank manager is very familiar with this risk, which is why they may want extra security from the directors that use property as security — particularly for property letting, trading or development companies. In recessionary periods property values may fall and banks can get nervous about the adequacy of their security. For property companies or for trading companies whose loans are secured primarily on property there is a risk of lenders demanding extra security. The bank may demand a revaluation of properties at such times and may even ask the customer to pay the cost of the valuer. There are cases of property investors who have good tenants, whose rents provide ample cover for the mortgage, being asked to repay part of it to compensate for lower property values.

So, what can you do? If you can afford to repay part of the loan then there is no issue — you can do that or you can call the lender's bluff — but if you can't then you are in a very difficult situation. If the property has fallen in value then another lender would offer terms that are no better. The first step is to look at the precise terms of the loan agreement. Does the bank have a right to demand a valuation or to review the loan and do they have any right to ask the borrower to pay? Unfortunately they often do have these rights and, if they don't, they may have a right to withdraw the loan under certain conditions. The local bank manager, with whom you have built up a rapport, often has no discretion in the matter. Offering additional security may be a better option than finding extra cash but may not always be possible. Anticipating the problem, if you know property prices have fallen, may give time to think of an alternative but, for a financially distressed company, there often is no alternative. Consider a sale and leaseback — it may be better to accept a loss on the sale but, at least, to repay the mortgage and to be able to continue trading. However, always take a critical look at the prospects for the business. It makes no sense to pay extra money into a struggling business or to sell its assets if neither act will resolve a fundamental trading problem.

What other things can you do to pre-empt possible problems?

- **Arrange an approved line of credit well in advance.**
- **Give personal guarantees to support borrowing.**
- **Use more than one bank or finance house.**

And what can you do if the bank is difficult?

- **Ask your accountants to intervene.**
- **Appeal to a higher level in the bank.**

Do not emphasise that your business will fail if the lender will not help. Whilst this is true of almost all businesses, it will nonetheless make your bank manager nervous.

Different types of finance

Part of a negotiation with a bank may be over alternative types of finance that it may find more acceptable e.g.

- **term loan versus overdraft;**
- **fixed-rate loan;**
- **asset financing;**
- **credit card finance.**

Generally banks will prefer a customer to have a term loan if their need for finance is long-term rather than short-term or seasonal. This provides a schedule of loan repayments and therefore convinces the bank that the risk is lower and repayment more assured.

At times of volatile interest rates or fears of higher rates in the future it may be a good idea to seek fixed-rate borrowing even if it is a little more expensive when it is taken out. Large companies can achieve this through financial instruments such as interest rate swaps but such instruments are not always available for smaller companies.

A bank may see asset financing as more acceptable than a working capital loan. This can be because of their internal processes but equally because the security relates to an identifiable asset.

Fixed or floating charge priority

When a business deals with more than one lender there is often a problem about security. Both want security over everything. This is not surprising in view of the tendency of value to evaporate when a business hits financial distress. Because the lender does not know how valuable their security will turn out to be they want extra, just in case. But then the bank does not want to finance a particular need and so the business turns to someone else who also wants security. The bank will insist on having a first charge, which means it has first bite at the assets. This leaves the new lender with a second charge, which may prove harder to get value from. This leads to an argument between the lenders which turns out to be your problem as well as theirs.

The outcome is usually a 'deed of priorities' which sets out who gets what and in what order, if the business becomes insolvent.

Dealing with bailiffs

The law relating to bailiffs is confusing and complicated and requires a book in itself to explain. And although the government has indicated it will reform this area, previous governments have said this and done little. Key points are summarised below but the most important point of all is to try to negotiate a settlement with bailiffs if they gain peaceful entry to your premises.

Different types of bailiff

The term 'bailiff' is not a protected term so anyone can set themselves up as one. A bailiff is just someone who is authorised by a creditor to collect their outstanding debt. There are a number of types:

- **Certificated. Some private sector bailiffs hold certificates from the courts that allow them to act on tax and similar matters. They must be 'fit and proper', pass a criminal records check, must post a £10,000 bond and are regulated by the courts.**
- **Private. There is no statutory control over these people so complaints, if criminal, have to be made to the police or through legal action for compensation. If they are members of an association, that will require them to have a formal complaints procedure.**

• **Warrant. The creditor has obtained a county court judgement but has still not been paid within 30 days so they can apply to the court for a warrant of execution. If they are based in another area, the court can forward this to the local court to execute. A notice of warrant will be issued to the debtor and, if payment is not made, a bailiff of the court can be sent to collect payment or seize goods.**

Bailiffs' powers

Bailiffs should provide identification or authorisation if asked. They do not have the right to forcibly enter premises except as outlined below.

Sheriffs and bailiffs rely upon ancient laws to obtain entry to property, such as open doors and windows. They (usually) cannot force entry and the debtor can simply close and lock all doors and windows where they could gain access. Knowing their limited powers, they may seek to obtain entrance by just walking in through an open door, asking to use the telephone etc. Of course, many business premises have open access. Any attempt to remove a bailiff from your property once they have gained peaceful entry is assault, and you could be taken to court for it.

Once inside, a bailiff will attempt to seize goods in order to sell them off at public auction to raise money to pay the debt that you owe. They will make clear an intention to seize items either verbally or by attaching a mark to them, or by touching them. This is sometimes called 'levying distress' or 'distraining upon goods'. The bailiff may take the goods immediately or take what is known as walking possession.

Bailiffs for the Collector of Taxes can get a warrant to force entry.

Walking possession

This is a legal agreement signed by the debtor and bailiff that acknowledges that items listed have been seized by the bailiff and must not be moved or disposed of without the bailiff's consent. He or she can return any time after five days have elapsed and take the goods unless the debt and bailiff's fees have been paid. For the debtor to remove or sell the listed assets after they are covered in this way is a criminal offence. If the bailiff has obtained a walking possession, he or she can force entry to recover the goods after the five day period

The advantage is that this gives time to pay or to agree a repayment schedule. The disadvantage is that it sets a daily fee rate that builds up until the debt is paid. It also permits, in the event of a default on the repayment agreement, for a further 'attendance to remove' fee.

It is also not usually possible for the bailiff to possess or remove goods that do not belong to the company but it is up to the occupant of the premises to prove the items belong to someone else. It is important to explain to the bailiff if particular items belong to another company or individual and why they are on the premises. Personal items or those covered by leases or higher purchase agreements should not be taken. The business will still have a liability to the finance company if their property is wrongly taken. Where items are subject to retention of title clauses, they still belong to the supplier if they have not been paid for in full. The bailiff should be alerted to this and, if possible, shown the supplier's terms of trade that specify retention of title.

If you have a debenture, this means that you have taken out a loan and, in return, have given the lender a charge over identified assets or over all the assets of the business. The document that sets this out is called a debenture. Whilst this does not mean that the lender owns the assets, bailiffs do not usually want to get embroiled in arguments with high street banks.

It is still possible to do a deal with a bailiff, after walking possession is in place. It may be possible to keep and use the goods whilst making regular payments but any default on such an arrangement could result in their removal without notice.

If a bailiff is calling, it is quite likely that the company is insolvent. As a minimum, it would be prudent to obtain professional advice to be sure it is not engaged in wrongful trading. Whilst locking doors and windows might keep a bailiff out, it has to signal to the directors that there is a serious problem and that something must be done.

Complaints about bailiffs

Bailiffs should not be aggressive or use threats or violence: this would be unlawful and the debtor can lodge a complaint against them.

To complain about a certificated bailiff, the debtor can apply to the court, which asks for the bailiff's response, which must be supplied within 14 days. If the judge is dissatisfied, the bailiff could be obliged to pay compensation or lose his certificate. This possible sanction provides a lever for negotiation without having to wait 14 days, which may be too long for a company in difficulties, and does not remedy the immediate problem. Approach the bailiffs in the first instance, laying out the complaint, and see if you can obtain satisfaction this way.

The most common grounds for complaint are:

- **excessive fees that do not meet regulations;**
- **aggressive behaviour;**
- **illegal levy on goods that do not belong to the debtor;**
- **irregular levy — goods have been properly possessed but sold despite payment of costs;**
- **excessive levy — seizure of goods to a greater value than the debt.**

Regulations on fees are complex and depend on the cause of the distraint: taxes, fines, county court and high court judgements will all attract different levels of fees.

Of course the big problem with taking legal action against bailiffs is that the need probably occurs when you are short of the funds to finance it. Do you have property or business insurance that also covers legal fees? Check the wording to see exactly what is covered.

Recovering excessive bailiffs' fees

A debtor has a right to original documents detailing fees that have been paid. If payment has been made but detailed original documents have not been provided, the debtor can send a written request for original documents outlining charges and visits. This is referred to as a Subject Access Request (S.7), which is pursuant to Section 7 of the Data Protection Act 1998. The bailiff company is required to comply within 40 days. If they fail to do so, it is wise to send a second letter giving them a further 7 days before taking court proceedings.

Your practical steps if a bailiff calls

If you can prevent a bailiff from entering your premises and seizing goods to sell, you have won a temporary respite but clearly a more permanent solution is needed. It may well be that a temporary respite will do the trick — a few days to gather in money from people who owe you a debt or to raise it from family or friends or from selling off assets. If you can't find a quick fix, though, you probably have three choices:

1. **Negotiate with the bailiff.**
2. **Negotiate with the creditor who has sent the bailiff.**
3. **Find an insolvency practitioner and go into administration or set up a Company Voluntary Arrangement (CVA) (these options are explained later on) . With bailiffs laying siege you may not have time to investigate alternatives... but you might.**

If the bailiffs fail this time, they will probably return or your creditor may try a winding-up petition. Any such actions will affect your ability to trade effectively so you must do something.

If the bailiff has entered and seized goods, you can try to negotiate a settlement, perhaps with time to pay. You will not be given very much time, so you will have to act quickly. If you can't find the cash, you will have to let them have the goods and manage as best you can. Try to negotiate a deal on what goods they take, so they leave items you need to trade with.

Credit ratings

What is a company credit rating? Rating firms calculate a credit score based upon many factors that are fed into a formula. The rating firm will also give an indication of the risk associated with each range of scores and some will recommend a level of credit to be given to a customer.

The theory behind this goes back to the 1930s when academics, using analysis of published accounts, tried to predict the probability of listed companies filing for bankruptcy within two years. In 1968 Edward Altman published a technique called the 'Z-score' that has been highly regarded and this was followed up with an amended technique applicable to private companies that used five accounting ratios.

The proprietary methods used by commercial rating companies will include, alongside the analysis of accounts, factors such as county court judgements, directors who have previously been associated with business failures, late filing of accounts etc.

The ratings are important to trading companies because they may be used by finance companies and also by potential suppliers to support lending or trading decisions. They may also be used by credit insurers who are used by those suppliers. In extreme cases a supplier may feel themselves unable to do business with a customer because they cannot get insurance for their debt and are unwilling to take the risk themselves.

Anyone who uses these measures should bear in mind that they are not always accurate. In the case of private companies, they may forecast business failure correctly 80% of the time, but they will also fail to predict failure or predict failure when companies survive. This may be because accounts can be misleading, even audited ones. It is more likely, however, to be due to the variability that is inherent in any statistical technique. The rating used by different rating firms may also differ, with one indicating it is safe to trade with a particular company whilst another takes an opposite view.

Elsewhere in this book I suggest that suppliers should make use of credit rating bureaux. How does this square with saying they are not always accurate? There is actually no contradiction. Even if they do not give certainty they may help to improve decisions. It is important for the user to understand that they may be wrong and not to use them blindly. The decision to extend credit always lies with the supplier in the end and the bureaux only supplies information that may be helpful.

Where a company feels it has been refused credit unfairly it may be possible to find the credit rating firm that has been used and to see the rating. Companies have a right under the Data Protection Act to see their rating but will have to pay for it. They also have a right to correct factual errors on a credit report, however, there is not necessarily a right of access to the credit scoring formula each firm uses.

There are companies that call themselves 'credit repair agencies' that claim to undertake services such as having County Court Judgements expunged from the records. There is no lawful route for doing this before they expire anyway [after six years] and such firms have been accused of operating a scam.

Retention of title

Companies that supply retailers, in particular, often include a clause in their terms of trade that retains legal title to their goods until they have been paid for. This is often referred to as a 'Romalpa clause' after a key legal case. It means that if the supplier is not paid on time, according to those terms of trade, they can send bailiffs in to the buyer's premises to seize the goods. In theory this is a quick, cheap and simple way to either obtain payment or goods that can be resold to recover the debt.

Although this seems quite straightforward, the devil is in the detail and many attempts to exercise 'retention of title' clauses have failed.

When the clause simply appears as part of the supplier's terms of trade on the back of an invoice, that may be insufficient. The terms will often say that by accepting the goods, the recipient also accepts the terms of trade but that may not be sufficient either. If, for example, the invoice incorporating the terms of trade was sent *after* the goods were accepted then the contract has been completed before the terms can have been agreed.

To make quite sure of a valid claim, many companies get the customer to sign and return a document setting out the terms of trade as an acknowledgement of accepting them. For the clause to be effective, it's important that the terms are:

- **in a contractual document signed by the insolvent;**
- **contained in any unsigned document incorporating contractual terms of which the insolvent knew, even if unaware of their effect;**
- **in a document which the supplier had done all that was reasonably necessary to draw the terms to the insolvent's attention prior to entering into the contract.**

The goods claimed must also be identifiable.

If the supplier cannot prove that particular goods belong to them, they cannot seize them. In order to ensure that goods can be identified, a supplier's terms of trade will often require the customer to keep their goods separate from those of other suppliers. However, raw materials cannot be seized once they have been worked on and incorporated into something else unless they can be easily detached without damaging the new item.

Regardless of the method used to enter into the contract any subsequent changes to that contract may be made in writing or orally but must be agreed to by both parties. It may be possible to backdate a change to the contract between buyer and seller but this must be agreed between the parties. It is unlikely to succeed if the customer is already insolvent. For example, when I was a director of a company that was in some financial distress, one of our suppliers asked us to agree to a retention of title clause that related not just to future purchases but also to past purchases. Agreeing to that could have been seen as an attempt to give fraudulent preference to this creditor at the expense of others.

When an insolvency occurs, the Official Receiver or an insolvency practitioner will usually ask the directors whether they are aware of goods that may be subject to retention of title. They will also ask the creditors this when asking them to submit their claims. They will then seek to decide whether such clauses are valid in the circumstances. They will check that:

- **the wording of the clause covers the particular goods or monies being claimed (the claim can extend to the proceeds of sale of particular goods);**
- **the clause has been incorporated into the contract of sale that exists between supplier and customer;**
- **any goods claimed can conclusively be identified;**
- **where the clause is not an 'all sums' clause, the claim relates to goods supplied under a specific unpaid invoice.**

If they dispose of goods that turn out to have a valid retention of title clause, the supplier will be entitled to the proceeds of sale and the Official Receiver or insolvency practitioner may be personally liable for any loss suffered by the supplier.

Winding-up petition

A winding-up petition is the most serious action that can be taken against a company. Typically a petition costs over £1,200 to issue, so the creditor who initiates this is serious in their intent to recover money, or is angry and wants punishment through putting the company out of business.

It is likely, at this stage, that trust has broken down between the company and its creditor; perhaps an agreement has not been adhered to, cheques have bounced or telephone calls have not been returned. Putting aside the motive of punishment, either the creditor believes the company is able to pay but does not want to, or that the company cannot pay but has assets that can be sold to clear the debt. However, it is still not too late to negotiate a solution that may give a better result to both sides.

If the debt is paid at this stage, it will have increased because of the costs incurred by the claimant. If you are served with a winding-up petition, you must take legal advice immediately. There may well be grounds for resisting the action. The court has very wide powers if the petition reaches a hearing, to:[4]

- **dismiss it;**
- **make an interim order;**
- **make any other order it sees fit;**
- **adjourn the hearing conditionally;**
- **adjourn the hearing unconditionally.**

If the petition is fair and indefensible, the petition hearing will (in due course) be published. At this stage, bankers will find out and will freeze the company's bank accounts to prevent any misfeasance or illegal acts by the directors. Landlords may find out and may commence action to forfeit leases. If the action is fair and indefensible, a petition hearing will be followed by the appointment of a liquidator.

Make very sure that all board and management actions in the period leading up to this point have been carefully recorded and that the assets of the business have not been disposed of. A liquidator can examine transactions and management action in the two years leading up to insolvency.

---

4 Insolvency Act 1986 S. 125.

CHAPTER 5
ALTERNATIVES TO INSOLVENCY

However bleak things look, there are alternatives to insolvency and to liquidation that can save the underlying business. Well, there are some alternatives that can be reached through using insolvency processes — and these are dealt with in the next chapters. But there are also some that can be arrived at without the destruction of the business: jobs can be saved, creditors can be paid and value can be rescued.

Saving a business depends on whether there is a viable enterprise hiding beneath the present financial difficulties. If the business is no longer viable, the only options are to sell the company or to liquidate it, which involves ceasing to trade and selling whatever assets can be sold. If the heart of the business is still beating, however, investigate the following options.

Company restructuring

It's pretty unusual for a restructuring of the finances of a company to be the sole way of solving its problems but it can at least provide a breathing space for other actions to be taken that can rescue the business.

One way of restructuring is to convert debt to equity so that interest and debt repayments are no longer made but the previous holders of the debt participate in the future potential of the business. This can happen when a business has issued loan notes or some similar form of debt to individuals or to financial institutions. Sometimes the owners of these loan notes can be persuaded that they will be better off swapping them for shares. This may arise if:

- **it is clear that the business will be unable to repay the loan or to pay the interest;**
- **the company balance sheet shows far too much debt in comparison to share capital so that the bank is concerned about the viability of the business. In such cases, even a slight dip in profits can make the company unable to service its loans. That drop into trading losses will very quickly result in a negative balance on shareholders' funds, which is one of the indicators of insolvency.**

By taking shares, the holders of loan notes will strengthen the balance sheet, as well as give the company a welcome break in which to recover and to benefit from that recovery. The shares may be special ones — often called preference shares — that have a right to a dividend, perhaps at a pre-agreed rate, in preference to other shareholders. Those holding the loan notes may be entitled to a percentage of future profits, or maybe the loan notes will be repaid or converted to ordinary shares. The rights involved can get very complicated.

Agreeing to take these shares may be far preferable to an alternative of not having loan notes, or not having interest paid on time. Also, depending on the rights associated with the new shares, the bank may view them as equity and not debt and, seeing a healthier balance sheet, may be willing to increase lending to the business.

Raise new funds

Sounds obvious, doesn't it? But it's worth considering again at these times, particularly if you can find a new angle to explore. This solution presumes the core business is viable and that a cash injection, whether to resolve short-term cash flow problems or to provide investment for new projects, will resolve the difficulties.

If raising money will leave the business with exactly the same problems but merely delay them, it is not a solution but rather a pause on the road to insolvency. Therefore the first step in raising new funds is to produce a recovery strategy.

The second step is to get to the point of implementing that strategy. Do you have enough working capital to cover immediate needs?

New funding can come from existing or new sources. The first port of call will always be to existing investors or banks, not least because this is the easiest route to follow. Existing funders can often block you from going elsewhere. A loan agreement with one financier may limit the total borrowing from all sources but, even if there is no constraint, it may be difficult for a new lender to obtain security without the agreement of pre-existing lenders.

Retailco had bought several properties with the help of loans that it had now almost repaid. It had some financial difficulties but believed these could be resolved by borrowing more and refurbishing its units. However, the existing lender was reluctant to lend more. A new lender was prepared to provide finance but wanted its mortgage to be a first charge on one of the properties. This required the first lender to release its charge. It refused to do this even though the security provided by the other properties was more than sufficient. There was a solution in this case, which was for the second lender to provide enough funding to repay the first lender.

New investors will not want to put their money into a business that is failing. However, there are many instances of businesses that are fundamentally sound but just have a short-term financial problem. These examples normally include businesses that:

• **are profitable but have run out of cash through overtrading;**

- have run into a single non-recurring problem e.g. a single large bad debt;
- can be restructured to create a viable business;
- started out with insufficient capital.

Start by writing a business plan. That concentrates minds on what matters. Every business plan is different and they differ depending upon what their purpose is. This one will have to address:

- what has gone wrong;
- how it will be corrected;
- how much investment is needed and for what;
- the risks;
- what payoff there will be to someone providing new funds.

Most businesses get into difficulty as a result of management failures. If you have made mistakes you need to persuade a lender or investor that:

- the existing team has learnt from this;
- new management skills have been recruited;
- organisational failures have been addressed.

Relationship failures are often at the heart of other failings. Is the management team working well together? If it is not, what are the issues and what can be done about them? There is no point seeking new funds until underlying problems have been worked out, because lenders and investors will soon discover them.

Sources of new funds

There are many sources of new funding, even for businesses in financial distress and even when there are existing lenders who have charges over the assets.

Asset refinancing

This is ideal for sectors such as manufacturing, engineering, print, construction and transport, which work with a large asset base. Refinancing these can provide a substantial injection of cash. A loan will generally be a percentage, ranging from 50 to 75% of an independent valuation. Assets already subject to finance can be refinanced, with the existing lender paid off as part of the process. Loans will usually be up to five years but can be less where assets are old or have a short economic life.

Mortgage or re-mortgage

Companies often operate from premises that have risen substantially in value and may not be encumbered with a mortgage at all or may have financing that is a relatively small percentage of their value. This presents an opportunity to re-mortgage properties and release cash.

Invoice financing

Banks will often offer invoice financing but there is a wide range of other providers. Factoring hands the entire collections process to the finance company whilst 'invoice discounting' retains control and the company borrows a percentage (often up to 90%) of their receivables based on various criteria, including the credit rating of the customers.

Trade finance

Trade finance companies advance money on the security of confirmed orders. Clearly they will be more cautious when a company is in distressed circumstances and there is a risk of non-completion. Nonetheless, this is a potentially valuable part of the financing portfolio where the pressure on a business arises from difficulty in financing larger orders.

Private investors

There are a number of brokerage firms that will match private investors or private equity firms with businesses that need help.

This action will usually be associated with a direct management involvement in the business and a dilution of the existing owners' equity stake. However, additional expertise may prove an added attraction rather than a penalty.

Sell assets

What about things you can sell? This may be property or equipment. If you can do without something, consider an outright sale but, if the property or piece of equipment is still needed, then what about a sale and leaseback? Instead of owning the asset, you still use it but pay a 'rental'. There are many finance houses that will enter into sale and leaseback transactions. The equipment generally needs to be fairly new so it can be resold if necessary and the length of the leaseback will have to be less than the economic life of the asset.

Sell part of the business

There are often activities carried out by a business that are not really at the core of what it does. For example, businesses that sell equipment will often sell maintenance or insurance alongside; or they may have a property management arm if they operate from many sites; or operate car fleet management if they have many vehicles on the road. They may have a fantastic website and design websites for third parties. Any of these may prove to be a viable business in its own right that can be spun off. Alternatively, one of these may prove to be the future for the business and it is the old business that spawned it that needs to be sold off.

However, do be careful not to react too quickly without careful consideration: sometimes what seems to be a peripheral activity is really critical to the operation of the rest of the business.

I heard an executive of a hotel chain on the radio describe his business as an e-commerce business with a hotel management activity on the side. Now I think he was exaggerating but, still, this is an example of a situation where you wouldn't sell off the website design and management activity, because it sounds like a core activity and not peripheral at all.

Sometimes this secondary activity needs time to build, separate and get ready for sale. Do you have time? Can something else be done to keep the whole business afloat whilst this is done? There may be a potential buyer out there who would be interested in taking the activity as it is and developing it into a significant standalone business. Of course they would offer a price that reflects the work they have to do but if cash is needed quickly is this a practical option?

The practicalities of selling a part of a business are very similar to those involved in selling the whole, which is dealt with in the next section.

Credit card financing

Smaller businesses faced with financial distress may use personal or company credit cards to borrow. This is an act of desperation because the interest rates are very high and the amounts that can be raised are likely to be small. However, there can be circumstances when it should be considered.

Tax benefits for investors

A bad investment remains a bad investment even if it is eligible for a tax break. However, if a rescue proposal is convincing but the prospective financial return is not quite good enough to attract the investor, an increase derived from a tax break may just tilt the balance.

Enterprise Investment Scheme (EIS)

The main UK tax benefit that can be offered to an investor in a struggling business is the Enterprise Investment Scheme. This will not be suitable if finance must be raised within days because it is more likely to take a couple of weeks to put one together. This used to be a simple scheme that a company's finance director could put together but to combat the growth of complex tax avoidance, a host of conditions and regulations have grown up that mean it will now generally be necessary to get professional advice.

EIS offers:

- **a 30% rebate on investment through a personal income tax allowance;**
- **tax-free capital gains after shares have been held for three years;**
- **losses that can be offset against income tax;**
- **capacity for investments of up to £1m.**

What kind of companies are eligible? The conditions change frequently, so it is sensible to check the current position. Broadly they are private, trading companies (not property or investment companies) below a size specified by employee numbers, balance sheet value and turnover.

Sell the business

Clearly it is not that easy to sell a business, particularly not one in difficulty, but it is worth thinking about.

Who might be interested?

- **Suppliers or customers?**
- **Competitors?**
- **Foreign buyer seeking entry into the UK?**
- **Someone to whom the business is worth more than it is to you?**
- **Turnaround investors?**

Either suppliers or customers may be interested in acquisition. The supplier faced with losing a significant channel to market may prefer to assist it through a difficult situation or to buy it outright. The alternative might be that they lose a substantial part of their own turnover either temporarily or permanently. Customers who depend upon the product or service you provide may, similarly, find it difficult to replace you.

Of course there is a risk in approaching a competitor. They may just contact all your customers or your staff and tell them you are in difficulty. They then try to win your business away and recruit your staff. Even inadvertently they may let slip that they are in discussions with you. Further, you will have to give them information and they may just talk to you to find out what they can but with no real intention of doing a deal. What can you do to protect yourself? The first step is to get them to sign a confidentiality agreement; and your accountants or solicitors should be able to supply one. This will prevent them from approaching your customers or staff and oblige them to keep any information you give them secret. But be aware that it is pretty hard to enforce these agreements in practice and this is particularly the case if you are short of time and money. The second step is to try to work out if they have money to conclude a deal. Thirdly, you try to limit what information you give and what access you allow to your staff, while you build up confidence in their intentions. Finally you require a quick answer. If they can't make an offer within a few days, maybe you move to plan B, or try to negotiate a deposit. However, if you need to do a deal you may have little choice but to take whatever risk is involved.

You need to judge whether it is likely to be worthwhile approaching a competitor. Is your business big enough to provide them with economies of scale or do you have a regional presence that would complete their network? Do you have a product that they would like to add to their range? An approach to a competitor may be worthwhile even for quite small businesses where that business wants a presence just where you are based or in the small market niche you occupy or even, in some instances, partly to acquire the team or even an individual who is part of your team.

Searching out a foreign buyer, or someone else who wants entry into your market, is a likely option for larger businesses. However, there are cases of large companies buying many smaller companies and combining them to achieve economies of scale.

A company I worked for called Staveley Industries bought up relatively small businesses involved in manufacturing non-destructive testing equipment. These small businesses were spread around the world and had sales of only two or three million pounds each but, combined, produced a substantial company. This achieved economies of scale by selling through one sales force and covering most of the important niches in the industry.

Why would your business be worth more to someone else than it is to you? A company that is buying up small businesses may achieve economies of scale; they might get better volume discounts from suppliers or be able to trade with lower percentage overheads. On the other hand your business might be worth more to a competitor just because they could shut it down and put all the sales through their business. Or it may occupy a property that may be suitable for profitable redevelopment in a few years — if you can't wait, maybe someone else can.

Turnaround investors may appear in the form of brokers who assemble an investor group or they may be private equity houses that have already raised funds to invest in interesting situations. The only real difference between a private equity firm that specialises in turnaround investments, and the rest, is the understanding that businesses in financial distress may need to act very quickly and need very rapid assessment and action from investors. This is seldom an option for a really small business because only private investors are likely to be interested in investments below a couple of million pounds. However, even here it may be possible to find one or more private investors who are interested in smaller investments.

Analyse again what you have to sell. For example, is there:

- **a significant property?**
- **a good customer list?**
- **supply contracts?**
- **any unusual expertise?**
- **a well recognised brand name?**
- **volume or locations to add to someone else's business?**

How should you approach people?

- **Contact specialists in selling businesses?**
- **Direct approach to existing business partners — perhaps through an intermediary?**
- **Advertise?**

The instant risk in putting a business up for sale is that customers, suppliers and employees get spooked. This is not just true for approaches to competitors, but to anyone. As discussed above, it is possible to insist that a potential buyer signs a confidentiality agreement but you probably don't have the resources to pursue them through the courts if they fail to comply with their undertakings.

Working for a public company that had suddenly lost the confidence of its bankers, we decided to sell various assets. One retail business had a division that sold computers from relatively small premises. The division was not profitable because it was being overtaken by big 'shed' operators. However, its premises themselves were of great value to a mobile telephone company that wanted to build its customer base. It was the early days of mobile telephones and this

> company was eager to build sales very quickly and then to sell their business to one of the bigger companies.
>
> They knew we were in difficulties: we knew they were in a hurry, and so a suitable compromise emerged.

Lessons

Think creatively about who might be interested in the business, its people or its assets — it might not be someone obvious.

Compound with creditors

Compounding simply means reaching an agreement with creditors. There are two approaches: a formal or an informal deal.

The informal approach

If you have one or two major suppliers, they may agree to help you through your difficulties rather than lose your business. For them to help you, they must believe that your business will survive and prosper, so it's essential that you produce a business plan to discuss with them. They already know you and so you probably don't need a full-blown business plan that details the usual contents (history, markets, management, competitors, strategy etc.). The occasion may call for just a quick summary of that but it *will* require four critical components (adding in anything else you feel may be persuasive):

- **An explanation of why there is a problem.**
- **A strategy for recovery.**
- **The current financial position.**
- **A financial forecast.**

The statement of current financial position needs to summarise:

- **Creditors. How much is owed to each and how overdue they are? Virtually any computer accounts system will produce**

this schedule of 'aged creditors'.
- **Secured lenders. Spell out the amount owed, any repayments overdue, security, and covenants, whether they have been breached or not.**
- **Statement of affairs. This usually sets out assets and liabilities of a business on the assumption that it is not a going concern. However, in this situation it is more appropriate to assume the business will be saved but to exercise an extra degree of conservatism when considering issues such as the realisable value of property and likely recoverability of overdue debts.**

The statement should also include a financial forecast, which needs to be realistic and persuasive. It needs to show how, with some help from the suppliers, the business will be profitable and will pay-off overdue creditors within a reasonable time. What a 'reasonable time' means will depend upon the circumstances. It is likely to be months or, at the extreme, a year or two. It will not, however, be as long as five years.

An essential part of the financial case is a cash-flow forecast. Be realistic and be conservative. If debtors usually pay in 30 days, allow a little extra time. If the result shows that you are able to pay creditors in 90 days, ask for 120. If things do go wrong, get in touch with creditors as soon as you can to keep them up to speed: clearly they won't be thrilled, but if you don't keep them informed, trust breaks down. This forecast is likely to show units of weeks but when in difficulties, a business should produce a daily forecast for its own use.

The help required from creditors is likely to mean paying off a part of the outstanding debt over an extended period. In some cases, a deal may be possible that entails the creditors writing-off part of their debt. In such circumstances they will invariably want to see a comparable sacrifice from the owners of the business and possibly from other suppliers. The wider the circle of creditors who have to take part in such a rescue the more difficult it is to arrange.

Another approach may be to consider asking a wide circle of suppliers to accept delayed or reduced payment. This inevitably raises a problem for future supplies and must be considered very carefully. Options include asking for:

- **deferred payment;**
- **payment of a reduced amount over a period;**
- **payment of a reduced amount immediately.**

In every case the creditor should be asked to acknowledge in writing that the agreement is in full and final settlement, which means it cannot be reopened once the company is past its difficulties. The creditor should also be asked to confirm their continuing willingness to supply on the same terms (or different terms you may agree).

The advantages of this informal approach are:

- **That it can be carried out within just a few days and without incurring heavy fees from professional advisers.**
- **An informal approach may allow a different deal to be struck with different creditors.**
- **It can be a way of avoiding adverse publicity.**

There are, however, risks too.

- **Creditors may react by stopping further supplies or by ratcheting up their debt recovery proceedings.**
- **Creditors may not keep the approach confidential.**
- **Many property leases include a clause that permits termination if the tenant compounds with its creditors...**

This is a typical clause:

"... or if the Tenant shall compound or make arrangements with the Tenant's creditors or shall suffer any of the effects of the Tenant or the Surety to be taken in execution or if the Tenant (being a corporation) shall enter into liquidation whether compulsory or voluntary (except for a reconstruction or amalgamation of a solvent company forthwith carried into effect) or if a receiver shall be appointed in respect of any part of the Tenant's undertaking or if an application shall be made or a petition shall be presented to the court for the grant of any administration order under the Insolvency Act 1986 or for any order of similar effect under any law relating to companies or if an administrator or administrative receiver or provisional liquidator shall be appointed or if the Tenant or the Surety (not being a corporation) shall become bankrupt or make any assignment for the benefit of his creditors or make any arrangement with his creditors for the liquidation of his debts by composition or otherwise..."

It essentially provides for the landlord to regain possession of a property in the event of any insolvency process or any informal deal with creditors. These clauses are not always enforceable but legal advice should be taken.

However, landlords may prefer to have a tenant in place rather than risk incurring a void period and losing some of the rent that is owed. The key to assessing this risk is to take a view of the property market and whether the landlord would be able to re-let quickly and, even, at a higher rent.

- **A deal may be harder to reach the more creditors that are involved.**
- **Reaching a deal may take a lot of management time.**
- **If it does not work it might then be harder to go the formal route.**

Company Voluntary Arrangement (CVA)

The CVA is the formal approach to creditors. Its key features and main differences from an informal arrangement are as follows:

- **All unsecured creditors are approached and, if an agreement can be reached with those whose claims amount to at least 75%, by value, of all the unsecured debts of the business, it is binding on all of them, including those who voted against or refused to participate.**
- **Whilst attempting to reach an agreement, there can be a moratorium on legal proceedings to recover debts — usually for 28 days.**
- **The arrangement is dealt with through the courts.**
- **A supervisor, who is usually a licensed insolvency practitioner, is appointed to work alongside the management.**

The directors of a company can apply for a CVA unless it is in administration or liquidation, in which case the administrator or liquidator may still do so. Even if the administration or liquidation process has been started it can still be worthwhile to pursue a CVA for all or part of a business. So, for example, an administrator can disclaim uneconomic contracts and leases or close parts of a business and then start a CVA process in the hope that creditors will get a higher return than from a piecemeal sale of assets.

The absolute condition for taking this route is that the business can be viable and can return to profitability. There are two scenarios where the CVA may work:

1. **The business has a short-term cash shortage but is otherwise profitable. This is where the economic model is viable but, perhaps through an issue such as overtrading, the failure of a large customer or a cost overrun on a single project, there is insufficient immediate cash.**
2. **The business has a faulty economic model but, given time to adjust, it has good prospects for future viability.**

In both cases, the forecasts will show that if the immediate gap can be filled, that future trading will produce sufficient surplus cash for the business to continue.

The CVA provides key components that can help this to happen. In the first place there is the all-important moratorium when creditors such as banks, landlords and suppliers are prevented from pursuing their legal remedies such as seizing goods. This breathing space can then be used to try to reach an agreement with creditors. The moratorium is only available to smaller companies, as defined by the Companies Act S382[5] and some companies may choose not to take it. The procedure without one may be quicker and less onerous, with fewer reporting requirements.

The business will probably need additional working capital to see it through to recovery. This may come from:

1. **existing or new investors;**
2. **the company's bankers;**
3. **cash generated from trading.**

In the first two cases, the investors or the bank will have to be convinced that the capital structure is viable, which will probably mean that creditors agree to write-off part of their debts. If the business can generate sufficient cash from trading to ensure it prospers, this will still probably entail at least a deferral of debts owed to creditors and probably some write-off. In most cases, unless there is a write-off of some of the debts, there will be insufficient incentive left for the management team, who may feel they are working for their suppliers with their own potential reward extended too far into the future. In some cases, the suppliers may convert some of their debt into shares in the company. These may have restricted or deferred rights to capital and dividends — it being important not to remove the

---

5 Turnover less than £6.5m, gross assets not more than £3.26m and no more than 50 employees.

incentive for management to work hard to make the business successful.

The second key aspect of the process is therefore that creditors agree to either write off part of the value of their debts or to defer their repayment. It may also be important to get their agreement to continue supplying the company as before. Whilst the 75% vote by creditors may bind the other 25% to the agreement to accept reduced or deferred payment, there is no way of forcing them to continue supplies.

As well as having a breathing space the business may need to make other adjustments, which could include changes to:

- **strategy;**
- **management;**
- **underlying cost structure.**

It may, for example, be necessary to shed staff, abandon or renegotiate leases on premises etc.

CVA process

There are three stages to entering a CVA. The first is informal and occurs when the company directors decide to investigate this course of action. It is therefore an appraisal stage and will normally involve discussions with a professional adviser. It culminates in the directors deciding to proceed and formally appointing an adviser with experience of CVAs, who is usually also a licensed insolvency practitioner.

The second stage leads up to the formal papers that will be filed at court and sent to creditors. It involves assessing the situation, determining that a CVA is both viable and the best option and drawing up the plans and forecasts to support the proposal. There will be:

- **a business plan and cash forecast;**
- **a statement of affairs;**
- **a proposal for creditors as to how the CVA will work;**
- **formal documentation.**

Since a formal proposal will result there will inevitably be discussions with key suppliers to get their support — there is no point in sending out a proposal unless you know in advance that it is likely to be passed. Of course this can be a difficult time because the company is probably under pressure from creditors with the possibility of suppliers refusing to supply, applications for county court judgements and winding-up petitions. Bailiffs may enter premises and bankers may decline to provide further finance.

The attitude of banks is critical because a CVA does not affect the rights of secured creditors. They can still withdraw lending or exercise their security. And the very act of reaching a deal with creditors is an act of default under most finance agreements. So persuading them that the proposal is viable and winning agreement to support the CVA, or finding another bank to take over, is a top priority.

Administration followed by CVA

Once it becomes known that a company is in difficulties and considering a CVA, might this spur one or more creditors to petition for a winding-up? The company can be protected by the court, using an administration order, while its directors and the administrator put together a plan for the Company Voluntary Arrangement.

If there is a risk of a creditor winding the company up or a landlord taking aggressive action then this is a powerful (but expensive) way of controlling them. Usually nobody will feel it is in their interests to do this while alternatives are being investigated but, nonetheless, it can be a risk. If it happens, the company can ask the courts for a delay in granting a winding-up order in order for the CVA to be agreed — the courts have some discretion. An alternative is to put the company into administration, or just to start the process, in order to give time for agreement.

Towards the end of March 2011, Oddbins, a retail wine seller, started the administration process, which automatically gives it a period of protection from its creditors. This period extends over the quarter day when its rents are due and prevents landlords from reclaiming properties when rent is not paid. The court hearing is set for some 10 days after the quarter day. In the meantime negotiations continue to agree a CVA. If these are successful, the administration hearing can be set aside.

As soon as a plan is approved by a nominee and filed with the court there is the possibility of a moratorium to protect the company (see below). The final stage is a creditors' meeting at which a vote is taken to approve the CVA.

The lead-up to producing formal papers could take anything from a few days to a month or two. The period between filing papers and holding the creditors' meeting is a minimum of 17 days (legal minimum notice to creditors is 14 days) but is usually around 21 days.

The company continues trading during the time the CVA is being considered — but only as long as the creditors' interests are being optimised and not prejudiced. If, for example, the company had to take on significant new debts in order to keep trading then this would probably constitute wrongful trading and directors could be personally liable. If, as is usually the case, new debts can be kept to a minimum and are with existing suppliers, then it can be argued that the position of individual creditors and creditors as a group is not made materially worse and the proposal will be to their advantage. As soon as this appears not to be the case, the company directors would have to cease trading.

The moratorium

The original legislation did not provide for a moratorium, which was added by subsequent amendments. So there remains an option to file for a CVA without the protection of a moratorium.

The moratorium is also only available for small companies, as defined in the Companies Act which specifies that a company meet two out of three of the following criteria:

- **less than £6.5m turnover;**
- **balance sheet total less than £3.26m;**
- **not more than 50 employees.**

It lasts only for a maximum of 28 days unless the court grants an extension and exists from the point documents are filed until the creditors' meeting.

During this period, the most important protections are a block on winding-up petitions or resolutions, appointment of an administrator or administrative receiver by a secured lender; enforcement of repossession; entry of bailiffs or entry by landlords. This gives the company time to try to get support for the CVA from creditors without anyone taking steps that would result in the company ceasing to trade.

However, the company will still be under pressure because it will not have additional bank cash and must make do with what it can get from trading. Suppliers may also refuse to supply further goods on credit, though options remain of cash on delivery, a very short credit period or some form of security.

Restrictions are placed on directors to protect creditors. Any invoices issued must contain the nominee's name and a statement that a moratorium is in force. The company cannot obtain more than £250 credit without declaring there is a moratorium. Property can only be disposed of with the nominee's consent and in the reasonable expectation that it will benefit the company. If the property is subject to security from a lender then the proceeds must be used to repay that security. The nominee must approve payment of any pre-existing debts, which must be for the benefit of the company.

The actions of directors can be challenged in the courts by creditors, which can result in a wide range of action including sanction against the directors.

The nominee monitors the company's affairs during the moratorium to protect creditors, and must withdraw consent to act if it becomes clear that the CVA will not be approved or if the company runs out of funds to trade. Notice must be given to the company, creditors and the court, and the moratorium ends.

As court cases have multiplied, the law has become more complex and the moratorium is sometimes seen as too cumbersome now. It is therefore used less frequently, pushing the onus back on the company to either reach agreement with all key creditors in advance, or to use the dual mechanism of an administration followed by a CVA.

The CVA proposal

The CVA proposal that can be put forward to creditors is not defined by the legislation so it can be very wide-ranging — it is basically just a private agreement with creditors that is given support by the law. This allows maximum flexibility to do a deal that can save the business and optimise the interests of creditors. The offer to creditors will usually be a percentage of their debt that may be as little as 30 or 40% and this will be paid over an agreed period that may be as long as five years — there is no limit in the legislation. At the end of the agreed period, any debts not repaid will usually be written off. The amount paid may be a proportion agreed at the outset, it can be a minimum plus a percentage of profits, and it can include some shareholding for creditors. Often existing or new shareholders will invest additional money. Sometimes the bank or other secured lenders may write off part of what is owed to them.

Note that the forecast must be persuasive, which means the scheme is probably not appropriate for businesses with irregular or uncertain income, since that makes it difficult to make a convincing case and hard to set clear targets with a fixed timeframe.

There have been cases where an initial CVA was established on the understanding that a review of progress would be necessary after a period, followed by a further creditors' meeting to revise the CVA or to abandon it and petition to liquidate the company.

The proposal must provide for a nominee who will supervise the implementation of the CVA. This person must either be an authorised insolvency practitioner or a member of a designated professional body that authorises their members for this purpose [see page 208].

The CVA creditors' meeting

The proposal for the CVA will be presented at the creditors' meeting but creditors may propose amendments. The final outcome must be approved by 75%, by value, of those voting on the day. Votes may be cast by proxy.[6] It must also be approved by 50% by value of non-associated creditors, those other than directors and associated companies.

It is quite common for creditors to propose and pass modifications to the CVA. Whilst they may see this as imposing discipline on the directors, it may have the disadvantage of reducing their incentive to make it work.

Secured creditors can vote only in respect of their debts that are not covered by the value of their security, except in relation to a proposal to adjourn the meeting, in which case they can vote the entire value of their debt. This is because they may be stopped from enforcing their security by a moratorium on the one hand, but on the other hand they do have security.

After these votes, there will be a shareholders' meeting to confirm the CVA. However, even if this vote goes against the proposal, the directors are still empowered to proceed because their duty, once the company is insolvent, is to the creditors and not the shareholders. To avoid the CVA, the shareholders would have to remove the directors, replace them with opponents and also demonstrate that the company is not insolvent. Members (shareholders) can apply to the court within 28 days if they feel

---

6 A proxy is someone authorised to vote on behalf of the person entitled to vote. This may be covered by an instruction to vote in a particular way or to use their discretion. Normally the organisers of the meeting must be informed in writing of the proxy arrangement at least 48 hours prior to the meeting. Often the organisers will provide a proxy service rather than creditors being obliged to send their own appointee.

the result of the CVA proposal and vote is unfair to them.

The chairman must report the outcome of the meeting to everyone who was sent notice of it within four days and, if the CVA is approved, notify the Registrar of Companies.

Challenging a CVA

Once a CVA is agreed, a disgruntled shareholder or creditor can still challenge it but only on one of two grounds:

1. **That it unfairly prejudices them — they have been treated differently from others or the effects are to damage their interests more than other shareholders or creditors.**
2. **That there was some material irregularity at the shareholders' or creditors' meeting or insufficient notice was given.**

The challenge must be registered within 28 days of filing the results of the creditors' and shareholders' meetings with the court. If the challenge is successful, the court has wide discretion as to the order it can make. For example, it can declare the CVA to be invalid or direct the holding of new meetings and another vote.

Disadvantages of a CVA

There are sometimes reasons why a CVA will not work and expert advice will be needed. Although intended to be simple, the law has become very complicated and the original provisions of the Insolvency Act 1986 have been changed by numerous amendments.

There are also potential disadvantages:

1. **If the CVA fails it is possible that the outcome could be worse than if the directors opted for a solution such as administration immediately. The indebtedness could be greater and therefore the claim on guarantors could be larger.**

2. **The company's credit rating will be adversely affected by a CVA, which could affect decisions by suppliers and customers. Though, of course, not as adversely affected as by an administration.**
3. **As noted above, creditors may modify the details of a proposed CVA at a creditors' meeting and this action, if not well judged, may make the scheme less likely to succeed. This emphasises the importance of winning support from creditors before the meeting.**

What happens during the CVA

Once the CVA is approved, the nominee usually is appointed supervisor of the scheme and the directors and officers of the company must hand over any assets included in it. This means that assets that are charged to secured creditors (such as banks) are not passed over to the supervisor. All creditors who were entitled to vote at the meeting as well as any unknown creditors are bound by the scheme.

The supervisor must:

*   **Keep records and accounts and report at least once every twelve months to the company, its members, creditors included in the scheme, the court and the Registrar of Companies;**
*   **Report any directors they suspect of criminal offences in relation to the moratorium or CVA.**

New debts incurred after the CVA commences can still be the subject of enforcement proceedings up to and including a petition to wind up the company. It is then a matter of the wording of the CVA whether the assets contained in it are available for these later creditors or are held by the supervisor on trust for the CVA creditors.

Reducing directors' liabilities

A CVA can be used to reduce director's liabilities for, say, rent by having the lease as part of the CVA. If the lessor accepts a programme of lower future rents and the directors have given personal guarantees, their liability may be reduced too. Although the lessor may prefer to call on the guarantee there can be circumstances where, depending on its terms, they will be better off accepting the CVA.

Complaints

Any interested party may apply to the court if they are dissatisfied with acts or omissions of the nominee or the supervisor. The nominee or supervisor may also apply to the court for directions in case of uncertainty.

CVA problems

A CVA is not the same as administration and, once agreed, the company is not insolvent. One of its key features is that it is far less public. There does not have to be a public announcement nor do invoices and correspondence reveal that the company is in a CVA. (Companies House will have to be informed and will have a public note of it, however).

Nonetheless it is undeniable that there is some stigma attached, even though the fact that creditors and the bank are supporting the company has to be a vote of confidence. How might key stakeholders react?

Staff

There is always a risk that key staff will leave and that it will be hard to recruit replacements. However, going into a CVA does imply a vote of confidence in the business by some important and impressive constituencies — namely the bank, suppliers and probably the tax authorities. It is important to communicate honestly and openly with staff in order to win their support too. If they are kept in the dark or misled, their confidence will fall and they will look for alternative employment.

Bank

Directors often fear that the bank will react badly to a planned

CVA, particularly if it has good security, perhaps with personal guarantees. However, if their security is preserved and the proposal is persuasive, they have no reason to 'pull the plug'. If they do so, they will lose a customer and their security may turn out not be as good as it appears. They know very well that in a receivership or liquidation, much of the value of assets evaporates. They are worth far more in a business that is continuing to trade.

It is generally best to present the bank with a proposal and one that has, at least, been discussed with creditors and seems viable. Informing them at an earlier stage has the disadvantage of uncertainty. They may be concerned that their security will be compromised if too much time elapses and will be reluctant to allow long before they exercise their rights. The case will be transferred from the company's normal relationship manager to the bank's recoveries team as soon as it becomes clear that there is a problem and knowledge of the business or a good previous relationship will have limited effect on decisions after a very short time.

Customers

As with staff, there is always a risk that customers will confuse a CVA with administration, will fear the business is just about to cease trading and that they'll take their business elsewhere. Again, if the business managers are open, honest and timely in their communication, the risk of losing customers is greatly reduced. Customers will abandon ship if they fear that the company's ability to supply good quality products and services will be impaired: if they are persuaded that business will continue as usual, there is no reason to take their custom elsewhere.

HM Revenue

The tax authorities are often the largest constituency who must agree, alongside others, to write-off part of their debt. They too have an interest in the continuation of the company because it is better for them to receive part of what is owed than none of it. They too are acutely aware that the bank usually has security and is paid first, that employees' rights come next and that there is often little left for the tax liabilities. They also know that the value of assets evaporates in a liquidation. It is therefore not a surprise that they support some 70% of proposed CVAs.

Common reasons for rejection include:

- **failure to give full disclosure;**
- **failure to treat all creditors in a class equally;**
- **no provision to pay all future taxes as they fall due;**
- **failure to meet obligations under a previous CVA;**
- **previous lack of compliance.**

Although the HMRC's Voluntary Arrangements Service aims to respond to proposals within seven days, more time should be allowed for potential negotiation over their response.

Problems with suppliers
Suppliers can agree to a CVA but still refuse future supplies on credit, which would leave the business in serious trading difficulties. An approach to win them around is to propose making payments for future goods a condition of the CVA which, if breached, would require the supervisor to wind up the company. Try offering accelerated payment or, if necessary to secure supply, cash on delivery together with measures to ensure retention of title can be successfully applied. Another approach is for the supplier to hold stocks and supply when they are needed, limiting their risk.

Failed CVA
The CVA will sometimes fail because the business is unable to meet the debt repayments that it promised. Even if the forecasts were very cautious and the proposal only called for a part of the cash generated to be used to repay debts, nonetheless things can still go wrong. Some may be associated with the CVA itself; customers, staff or suppliers may be lost. The same range of risks that affect any business still applies to the CVA.

There is still the option of going back to creditors and revising the CVA, though some credibility may have been lost. Nonetheless, if the business still looks viable in the long term, a revised deal may still look more attractive than the alternatives. This revision may involve amendments to the terms of a CVA or even a new CVA that covers new debts that were not previously included, perhaps because new suppliers have been brought in.

The alternatives are some form of winding up. The ability of a secured lender such as a bank to appoint a receiver is unaffected by a CVA. If covenants have been breached or repayments are in arrears, a lender still has the right to appoint a receiver. Indeed the lender will often have the right to ask for their money back at any time, particularly from a company in CVA. If it is clear, therefore, that the company is failing to reach its targets, the bank can lose confidence, which can result in foreclosure. The supervisor who is looking after the interests of creditors can apply to the court for a termination of the CVA if agreed repayments are not kept up. And new debts, incurred after the CVA was agreed are not covered by it so, if they are overdue, action can be taken by creditors to recover them.

The end of the CVA

There is no duration for a CVA prescribed in the legislation, although a CVA will usually run for several years. The duration will usually be part of the CVA agreement. At the end of the agreed period, or when the agreed debts have been paid, the supervisor issues a completion certificate and the business emerges from CVA status. The unsecured debts that were frozen in the CVA and were not repaid during it are written-off at this point and the directors revert to running the business in the interests of its shareholders.

CVA costs

The total costs of a successful CVA are generally less than a receivership or administration, not least because the business continues to be managed by its directors rather than by an administrator.

In addition to lower fees, the company continues to trade and therefore avoids the evaporation of asset values that occurs during insolvency processes. The costs of a CVA comprise court fees, the expenses of the supervisor who looks after creditors' interests during the process and the expenses of the adviser, who helps to put the deal together.

CHAPTER 6
TYPES OF INSOLVENCY AND TERMS USED

Sometimes there is no alternative and the best solution is to pursue one of the insolvency options. If this is the case, there are some preparations that can be made.

Preparing for insolvency

How can you prepare for insolvency? Well, you are severely limited. You can't, for example, transfer assets from a sinking business to your own use. Not only is that theft, but the liquidator will pursue you for restitution and there may be a criminal prosecution. The line between what you can and can't do may be a difficult one, but there are some sensible things you can do as you become aware of the increasing risk, as long as the threshold of insolvency has not been crossed. If there is any doubt about a course of action you want to take, it is essential that you take professional legal advice. You might want to:

- Take personal copies of important documents, contacts and key data. Of course these are owned by the company and a contract of employment may preclude your use of confidential data, but there may not be anyone who would object in a liquidation. On the other hand, if the business were sold as a going concern, a buyer might object.
- Try to pay off any outstanding loans owed by directors to the company. A liquidator will pursue these if they are

outstanding and trying to repay them gradually may be easier.

- It is likely that a business in financial difficulty will tend to pay its critical suppliers before its less important ones (unless the unimportant ones press really hard), because they are necessary to being able to continue trading. These may also be the suppliers you would need to resurrect the business.
- Pay off some bank debt rather than creditors in order to reduce the consequences of personal guarantees being called in. This can result in an action for restitution by a liquidator. However, if it occurs well before an insolvency and in the normal course of business then it surely is not a preference.
- Claim your business expenses. That may sound trivial in the context of what else will be happening and the liquidator could well seek to reclaim them from you but, generally, they will be small; and, if you don't claim them back before liquidation, you won't get them afterwards.

You can't delay an insolvency to enable you to pay one more month of the payroll or to pay a particular creditor: that would certainly amount to wrongful trading. However, this is not an exact science and there may be occasions when it is not absolutely clear when the prospects for recovery have disappeared. Again, if in doubt, take professional legal advice.

It is important to have up-to-date board minutes and minutes of executive meetings. These will demonstrate that everyone acted properly and that it was reasonable to trade, up to the point when the decision was taken to the contrary.

Administration

What are the key components of administration?

Administration protects the assets of a company from creditors while the administrator tries to sell assets, or compound with creditors or sell the business. Virtually all recovery actions by creditors are halted. The objective of the administrator is to achieve the best possible deal for creditors. The interests of shareholders are not the prime concern, nor are employees, although this can be complex as they are also likely to be creditors.

Before accepting appointment, and to give a reasonable likelihood that it will be worthwhile and a better option than immediate liquidation, the administrator needs to consider three things:

1. **The company must be a reasonable size;**
2. **The company must have reasonably predictable cash flows;**
3. **The company must be able to forecast profitability.**

At that point in time, there must be an insolvent position, or contingently insolvent position, and the directors think that a hostile creditor will seriously affect the future trading possibilities. This is often a landlord or the Crown creditors.

The administration process requires a licensed insolvency practitioner (IP) to act as the administrator appointed by the court. The court appointed administrator takes over the management of the company and takes responsibility for restructuring the company or business.

If the company has little in the way of assets, poor cash flow and no future creditors, voluntary liquidation is probably more appropriate than administration.

There are two types of application to the High Court. There is the 'without court order' appointment route for holders of qualifying floating charges and the company itself or its directors — this is quick and does not need a court application or hearing. But sometimes it is better to still make the second type of detailed application which asks for a court hearing.

Who can appoint an administrator?

Companies and directors can appoint an administrator quickly with the IP's guidance. This does not require a court order: it requires a fax to be sent to the court with the appropriate forms.

Clearly, the IP must have done some work to establish if the company is insolvent, if it should go into administration, what the process will involve and the planned outcome. In many cases a bank effectively initiates administration because they will invite the directors to appoint an administrator.

Where a company is already in liquidation or in a CVA, the proposed administrator must obtain a court order empowering him or her to proceed.

No administration order will be granted unless the holders of all qualifying floating charges have been given five days clear notice of the company's or directors' intention to appoint an administrator.

The floating charge holder (usually a bank) has the right to step in and appoint its own choice of administrator but they tend not to do so when they are owed less than £200,000. Nonetheless, it is possible for the board to decide to appoint an administrator and for the bank to reject them and appoint its own from its list of recognised and approved IPs. If your chosen IP is not on the bank's panel there will not, generally, be a problem if it looks as though the bank will be paid in full.

Banks themselves can appoint an administrator if they hold a qualifying floating charge under new debentures granted after 15th September 2003 (or renewed after that date to accommodate the legislation). If the bank holds an older debenture, it can appoint an administrative receiver. The administrator they appoint still has a duty to act in the interests of *all* creditors not just on behalf of the bank or other floating charge holders.

There must be one (or two) of three 'objectives' for the administration. The proposed administrator must apply to the court to be appointed and state which of the following three possible objectives is their main focus:

1. **To rescue the company as a going concern. This may mean that the company proposes a pre-pack or administration followed either by a Company Voluntary Arrangement or a scheme of arrangement.**
2. **To continue trading temporarily and trying to sell some**

or all of the business as a going concern. This can only be done if the administrator can fund trading and believes they can achieve a better result for the creditors as a whole than would be obtained through an immediate winding-up of the company.

3. To collect and sell the assets for the best price to make a distribution to secured creditors and others. This is the objective if neither of the first two objectives is possible.

In cases where speed is essential in making the appointment, the rules include a provision that will allow for the filing of a notice of appointment during times when the court is not open for business. Typically this is by fax.

The filing of such a notice will bring into effect an interim moratorium on insolvency proceedings and other legal processes being taken against the company. In this moratorium, no creditor can start liquidation proceedings or send in bailiffs or exercise security without the leave of the court. This is unlikely when the court has effectively ratified the administrator's appointment. The court will want to have as much information as possible to ensure that the application for administration is correct and appropriate.

Administration sale

The company can enter administration to enable it to be sold. This can happen when it is under severe pressure with threat of legal action from creditors, or the bank, demanding repayment. The company is probably insolvent but it has a viable business. The board believes that a sale could be achieved but the company needs to be protected while this is done.

An administrator is appointed who will run the business for a period of, say, one to two weeks (just short of the 14 days before the administrator must adopt or disclaim contracts of employment). In that time, the business will be marketed.[7] A

---

7 Insolvency guidelines (Statement of Insolvency Practice 13) require the administrator to be seen to market the business for sale.

professional valuer will be hired to value all the assets, including fixed assets, stocks, debtors, goodwill, intellectual property etc. In some cases this valuation may have been obtained before the application to the court for administration.

If there are no higher offers — after advertising the business — then, in an agreed period, the directors of 'Oldco' can buy the business provided the valuations are met and the administrator believes this is the best deal available for the creditors.

Whether sold to former directors or to a third party, TUPE[8] regulations generally apply and therefore all employees rights move across to Newco. In some cases this can cause problems if the buyer finds it has acquired employees whose pay, pensions or other rights are better than those of its other employees. There is no easy solution to this since changing those rights or making workers redundant can lead to claims for wrongful dismissal as well as claims under TUPE legislation. An alternative of levelling up the pay and conditions of other workers may be an expensive option.

'Oldco' is then liquidated.

What happens when an administrator is appointed?

At the moment when an administrator (or liquidator) is appointed, three important things happen:

1. **The company is protected from legal process by creditors.**
2. **The bank account is frozen — this happens the moment the bank is aware of the appointment, when the five days notice is given.**
3. **The directors no longer have powers to act.**

During the five day notice period given to floating charge holders, the first two of these conditions is in place yet the directors can still act and can still trade, even though they will be unable to make payments (because the bank will have frozen the account).

---

8 Transfer of Undertakings (Protection of Employment) Regulations 2006.

They will generally not be able to place orders because that would incur a debt that they know cannot be paid.

Once the administrator is appointed, they will seek to assess the situation quickly and to decide whether to continue trading. They will also decide quickly what to do with the business. If they continue to trade, they will open their own bank account for the business and will often retain the directors to assist them.

Administration process

The administrator is required to do everything as soon as reasonably practicable. Initial proposals must be circulated to creditors within eight weeks of appointment, an initial creditors' meeting held within 10 weeks of the company entering administration and the creditors must be given at least two weeks' notice of the meeting. This can be extended with the creditors' consent and/or by the court if the administration is complex and information cannot be assembled within this period.

The administrator's proposals will include the details of appointment and the circumstances leading up to it, as well as how the purpose of administration will be met, including how the administration is expected to end.

Upon appointment, the administrator will require one or more of the current or former directors or company officers to provide a statement of the company's affairs, which they will be paid to produce, and these sums, as well as reasonable expenses (such as professional valuations) are a permitted expense of administration. The administrators may provide the specialist expertise themselves but, if not, any company officer carrying out the task should be sure to get written confirmation from them, in advance, of what they consider a reasonable expense.

Note that the officers of the company, which includes directors and senior managers, have a duty to assist the administrator — if required — to provide, within 21 days, a statement of affairs of the company detailing:

a. **particulars of the company's assets, debts and liabilities;**
b. **the names and addresses of its creditors;**
c. **the securities held by them respectively;**
d. **the dates when the securities were respectively given;**
e. **such further or other information as may be prescribed.**[9]

Failure to co-operate in producing a statement of affairs can lead to a substantial fine and disqualification from acting as a director. Other directors or officers may be retained or their contracts disclaimed at this time.

A copy of the statement of the company's affairs, or a summary of it, must be attached to the administrator's proposals. A copy will also be filed with the Registrar of Companies for placing on the company's public file. However, if information included in the statement of affairs is commercially sensitive, the administrator can apply to court to have the statement, or the relevant part of it, withheld.

Creditors' meetings

The administrator will send out proposals to creditors. Included with each creditor's copy of the proposals will be an invitation to the initial creditors' meeting, at which the creditors vote on those proposals and whether to accept them. The administrator is not required to hold a meeting if:

• **it is clear there will be no payout to unsecured creditors;**
• **the company is not insolvent.**

The administrator can also act before the creditors' meeting if haste is essential to obtain the best return for creditors. As discussed elsewhere, value drains from a business in administration very quickly, and a quick deal may provide a much bigger return than one that is delayed. This is particularly the case if the administrator does not have funds to trade the business as a going concern

---

9 Insolvency Act 1986, S. 47.

yet an interested buyer makes an attractive offer. Usually, in such cases, the administrator will try to contact the largest creditors to explain the situation and why speed is necessary, and to get their informal support.

The business of the creditors' meeting can be conducted by correspondence, although if 10% or more of the unsecured creditors (by value of their claims) demand a meeting, the administrator is still required to call one.

The proposals can be accepted (by a majority vote, measured by value of claims), modified and then accepted, or rejected. In the case of rejection, the administrator is required to report that fact to the court and seek further directions.

Following the initial creditors' meeting, and any subsequent meeting of creditors, the administrator is required to send a report of the outcome of the meeting to the court and to the Registrar of Companies for the company's public file.

A creditors' committee of between three and five people can be formed if the creditors require it. The administrator then manages the company's affairs, business and property in accordance with the proposals that have been agreed by the creditors and in consultation with the creditors' committee.

The administrator must send regular progress reports to the creditors, the court and the Registrar of Companies covering each six-month period from the date of administration until it ends, or until he or she ceases to act. These will provide full details of the progress of the administration to date, including a receipts and payments account (or what cash has been received and paid out) and any other relevant information for the creditors.

End of administration

The administrator is appointed for a period of one year, although this can be extended by the consent of the creditors and/or by the court.

Disadvantages of administration

The directors are not in control of the business and an offer from a third party may lead to their removal as directors. All orders or payments must be ratified by the administrator or his or her staff. Tax losses can be lost if no CVA is proposed.

Although the directors or shareholders may want to salvage what they can by buying part or all of the business, another buyer may buy the assets if they offer more.

The process is very public:

- **All correspondence (invoices, advice notes, orders, emails, websites, letters) must say XYZ Co. Ltd (In Administration). Customers and suppliers therefore become aware of the insolvency.**
- **The appointment must also be advertised in the *London Gazette* and in any relevant local or national newspaper the administrator thinks appropriate to ensure that the appointment comes to the notice of the company's creditors.**

Although the bank will usually agree to accept the company's administrator, they do sometimes appoint their own, which may present a risk to the director's position if they want to buy the company.

The costs for this procedure can be high and increase the longer administration proceeds. This is because the administrator and their team will either run the business themselves, or more likely will shadow and approve all actions by company management.

TUPE applies to Newco, so the new company cannot remove employees and must adopt their contracts. This can be a problem when planning to cut costs in the new company.

Financing continuing trading during the administration period can be difficult unless adequate resources are available or new funds can be introduced. The administrator will never be willing to accept the personal liability that would go with trading without such funding. One way around this is for the management team who propose to buy the business to be retained by the administrator to manage it during this period, but they will have to fund the trading and account to the administrator for stock that is sold.

Advantages of administration

- All legal actions are stayed by the process.
- It stops the financial position getting worse and putting directors at further risk.
- It can be very quick and cost effective if an 'administration pre-pack' is used properly. [See page 131]
- Protection from creditors can allow the administrator a reasonable time frame (the eight week period) to negotiate a deal to achieve the objectives, thus providing some protection for jobs and economic activity.
- It is possible for the administrator to appoint directors or managers to run the company, which is usually preferable to using the administrator's staff. The incumbent management already knows and understands the business and generally costs less than outsiders who have to learn and who must support another corporate overhead.

Administration followed by 'better result'

The company is protected by the court while the administrator runs the business for a while to see if anyone will buy it as a going concern. However, many administrations turn into what is effectively a longer form of liquidation. The administrator does not have to get the bank's permission to take fees, as would be required in a liquidation.

This can be a powerful tool, though, if the company comprises a mixture of poorly performing and good parts that can be sold to a new owner. Under the protection of administration the parts that cannot be saved can be closed down and their assets sold whilst the viable elements can be saved.

Administration 'pre-pack'

See under 'Using administration to save your business' (see Chapter 7).

Receivership

A receiver is appointed by a floating charge holder — this is typically a bank but some other creditors may have security, such as landlords.

The company borrows from a bank and, in consideration for providing the loan, the bank requires security. Normally the company will sign a document called a debenture, which outlines the rights of the lender in the event of a default or breach of conditions of the loan agreement (a separate document). An event of default may not just be limited to non-payment but can include distraint by bailiffs, or the appointment of an administrator or similar insolvency practitioner. A receiver can coexist with a liquidator or administrator.

The debenture will provide for a charge over the company's assets.

- **A fixed charge relates to immoveable property and equipment, called fixed assets. This charge will be registered at Companies House and the company is prevented from disposing of any of it without the permission of the lender. If they do so regardless, the purchaser will not acquire good title. If there is more than one lender then they may have an equal right to seize the assets if there is a default (referred to as ranking *pari passu*) or one will have a first charge and another a second charge. Their respective rights may be set out in a 'deed of priorities'. Assets will be sold to satisfy the first charge and, if there is any money left over it will be passed on to the second charge holder.**
- **A floating charge (also registered) relates to the current assets such as stocks, work-in-progress and debtors that the company needs to trade. Clearly the business cannot be required to get permission to sell these because they are part of day-to-day trading. So the charge is said to 'float' over the assets. If the business becomes insolvent the charge 'crystallises' and the lender can seize control of stocks and debtors, for example.**

Banks often have both fixed and floating charges. If the assets covered by the fixed charge are more than sufficient to cover the loan it is advisable for the borrower to try to resist the addition of a floating charge. Having both can create extra problems for a company in the event of insolvency.

In the event of default the debenture holder can:

- **demand the default or breach of covenant is rectified;**
- **appoint investigating accountants (usually paid for by the borrower) to determine how secure the loan is and what is the best route forward;**
- **demand formal repayment of the loan without notice (via a letter of demand);**
- **appoint a receiver to administer and receive the company's assets.**

The receiver has a duty to collect the bank's debts only and is not generally concerned with the unsecured creditors' or shareholders' exposure. This means that despite their duty to obtain market prices for whatever they sell, in practice the unsecured creditors may not do as well in this form of insolvency.

Steps to receivership

The lender can ask for any or all of the following as it becomes concerned about the performance of the account:

- **A reduction in its exposure.**
- **Increased security from the directors or shareholders. Usually this takes the form of personal guarantees to support the security that the company has given through the debenture.**
- **New capital to be introduced by the shareholders. This may be the same as asking for a reduction in bank exposure because it may take this cash to reduce the borrowing.**
- **A new business plan along with regular (possibly enhanced) financial reporting.**

• **For the company to consider receivables finance (factoring) to remove its borrowing and move to a factor, which is often the bank's own factoring company.**

If still not satisfied with the performance of the business, or the control of the directors, and concerned about its exposure, a lender will ask for investigating accountants (or reporting accountants) to look at the business. Normally this is a large firm of accountants who send an individual or a team into the business to ascertain:

• **whether the business is viable if the short-term difficulties can be overcome;**
• **whether the bank's exposure is covered in the event of a failure;**
• **what the assets of the business are worth on a going-concern basis, and as a break-up in a forced sale;**
• **what future lending is appropriate.**

If the accountants believe that the company is at serious risk of failure and that the banks may lose money in that event, they will usually recommend the appointment of a receiver or administrator. This takes the form of the lender requiring the directors to 'request the bank to appoint a receiver'. In reality the directors probably have no choice if the bank demands immediate repayment.

Fixed charge receiver

There is a special form of receivership available when the lender's security is simply a mortgage over property, without a floating charge. He or she is known as a 'fixed charge receiver'. Unlike other insolvency appointments there is no requirement for the receiver to be an authorised insolvency practitioner and chartered surveyors are often appointed. Their powers are largely set out in the mortgage document, though they also have the limited powers set out in the Law of Property Act 1925, to receive rents and to insure buildings.

This kind of receiver is not required to report to creditors and so they represent a simpler, cheaper procedure than administration. They also do not have the same powers to demand information from directors and others that an administrator does.

Their authority is only over the property or other asset that provides the security for the charge and, if it is not essential for trading, the company can continue to trade. An example would be a property development business that has given a lender a charge over a particular development. The failure of that development and the exercise of that charge may not prevent the company from continuing to trade. There are a couple of 'ifs' to think about.

- **If the value of the asset is insufficient to cover the debt it is still possible for the lender to exercise any separate floating charge that it has or to take the same steps that any other unsecured creditor would take and to petition for a winding-up of the company.**
- **If the rest of the business is insolvent, the directors would still be obliged to act to protect creditors' interests.**

The publicity may be less and there may be no need to deal with preferential creditors. The whole procedure is cheaper.

The receiver's role and powers

The detail of what a receiver is empowered to do is set out in the debenture document. It may include taking, defending or settling legal actions; carrying on business; mortgaging property; committing to new obligations.

A receiver will move quickly to ascertain the prospects for the business and decide whether to sell some or all of the assets, the business as a whole, or to continue to trade to achieve a better deal. The need for speed results from the fact that values deteriorate quickly in administration or receivership [see page 132], and because the receiver will have to adopt employment contracts 14 days after appointment.

- **A receiver may dismiss directors and employees.**
- **A receiver does not have to consider representations from the directors.**
- **Preferential debts (employees' claims for arrears of pay and holiday pay, for example) must be paid first from any floating charge collections.**
- **If a deal is to be done with directors, the receiver must first advertise the business and its assets for sale to be able to demonstrate that it was the best available deal.**
- **A receiver must investigate the conduct of the directors of the business and file a report with the Department for Business, Innovation and Skills**

Receivership is a brutal and unsubtle process: the company is rarely saved in its existing form and the process rarely results in a restructuring and emergence as a strengthened business. This is partly because the focus of the receiver is simply on recovering the lender's money and partly because receiver's costs are high. In practice, unsecured creditors seldom receive a significant proportion of their money back and often they lose a valuable customer. As discussed elsewhere [Chapter 7], the value of assets evaporates, customers and suppliers are lost, employees leave and it is hard to resurrect the business even in a diminished form.

Alternatives such as a CVA or administration, particularly with a pre-pack, are more likely to result in a re-emergence of the business and more value may be saved.

However, where resurrection is not a possibility and, particularly where the directors have lost effective control, the receiver has the power to act quickly and decisively to bring the insolvency to a conclusion. The bank may recover all of its money, preferential creditors will often see their debts repaid by the receiver. The directors, while losing their investment and their employment nonetheless are freed from the anxiety of the company's problems and can move on.

Administrative receivership

This procedure is only valid for floating charges that were created before 16th September 2003.[10] For a company that has such a charge in place, the lender can appoint an administrative receiver, whose prime responsibility is to the charge holder and not to all creditors (as would be the case for an administrator).

The appointment of an administrative receiver does not create a moratorium and creditors, including landlords, can exercise their rights.

Members' Voluntary Liquidation

A Members' Voluntary Liquidation (MVL) is available only where the company is able to pay all debts (including the costs associated with winding up) within 12 months of entering liquidation. The directors will have to make a statutory declaration to this effect. The shareholders can vote in a general meeting or, for small companies, in writing to wind up the company and appoint a liquidator. The advantage of this approach is that it can be quick, a liquidator can be appointed immediately and can be chosen by the shareholders.

If it turns out that the company is not solvent after all, the liquidator will call a meeting of creditors and it becomes a Creditors' Voluntary Liquidation.

Section 110 scheme

Under Section 110 of the Insolvency Act 1986 one or more businesses of a company in MVL can be transferred to a new company, or companies, in return for shares in the new companies. These shares are then distributed to the shareholders of the original company. This procedure can be used to restructure a business, perhaps:

• **where shareholders want to separate their interests — so after the process the shareholders can swap or sell shares between themselves;**

---

10 Enterprise Act 2002.

• where part of a business is high-risk and part low-risk the shareholders can arrange things so that the failure of one will not bring down the other;
• to enable part of the business to be sold with the proceeds going directly to shareholders.

In addition to placing the company into MVL, the section 110 scheme must be approved by a special resolution of the shareholders. Any shareholder can object to the liquidator within seven days and require the liquidator to either halt the scheme or purchase their interest in the company. For this reason it is normal for the general meeting to approve the section 110 scheme to be held at least a week before the meeting to approve the liquidation.

A bank or a landlord may also be able to prevent such a scheme proceeding, depending upon the detailed provisions of their debenture or lease document respectively, because it could be used to try to remove assets from a business where a bank or landlord may have a claim in future.

Creditors' Voluntary Liquidation

Either at the end of administration, or where there is not enough to be salvaged to justify administration, an insolvent company will be liquidated. This is the process of closing a business and disposing of its assets and paying whatever sums are raised to creditors. Frequently creditors get very little in this process, with the fees associated with the process consuming most of what is realised. A Creditors' Voluntary Liquidation is the normal route for an insolvent company to become liquidated.

Unless the business is already in administration or in a CVA, the directors will agree that there is no prospect of saving the company as a going concern and will call an extraordinary general meeting of the company. At this shareholders' (members') meeting, the directors will report that the company is insolvent, that there is no reasonable prospect of paying existing creditors in full, or in reaching an agreement with creditors to allow the business to continue; they will report that it would be wrong to take further credit and will advise the shareholders that the company should voluntarily enter liquidation.

The prospective liquidator, who is a licensed insolvency practitioner, conducts a quick investigation into the affairs of the company and calls the creditors to a meeting. This is done by placing an advert in the *London Gazette* and in two local newspapers calling the meeting and writing to all known creditors inviting them to submit a claim for their debts. The liquidator is then appointed by the creditors at a creditors' meeting.[11]

The procedure for liquidation runs as follows.

- **The directors are generally advised by a Licensed Insolvency Practitioner that liquidation is the best solution.**
- **Trading will generally cease immediately.**
- **Meetings of shareholders and creditors are called.**
- **The creditors' meeting is advertised in two local newspapers and the *London Gazette*.**
- **The meetings must be convened on at least seven days notice with good practice being to give at least fourteen days notice.**
- **The creditors' meeting usually takes place just after the shareholders' meeting. If it is necessary to place the company into liquidation immediately without giving notice, the creditors' meeting can take place up to fourteen days later.**
- **At the shareholders' meeting, a Special Resolution is passed to cease trading and to place the company into liquidation. An Ordinary Resolution is passed nominating the liquidator. Could the shareholders reject this proposal? Yes, but the directors would almost certainly feel obliged to resign and shareholders would have to appoint new directors.**
- **At the creditors' meeting, a statement of affairs and a report on the history of the company and causes of failure**

---

11 Insolvency Act 1986, S. 98.

is presented to the meeting. Creditors may question the directors (although in practice few creditors attend) and either confirm the liquidator's appointment or, occasionally, substitute their own choice. If sufficient creditors are present, they can elect a creditors' committee, with between three and five members, to monitor the activities of the liquidator during the course of the liquidation. This will monitor the liquidator's fees, the sale of assets and the liquidator's investigation into the director's conduct, which is then reported to the Secretary of State.

The liquidator's four main tasks are to:

1. convert the assets of the business into cash;
2. adjudicate the claims of the creditors;
3. investigate and report to the authorities upon the conduct of the officers of the company (which includes both directors and any shadow directors);
4. make payments (where monies are available) to creditors.

However, they will also deal with administrative matters such as liaising with the tax authorities, terminating contracts, delisting the company from the Companies House registers and having it dissolved, which means it ceases to exist.

The company directors are required to:

• provide information about the company's affairs to the liquidator and to meet the liquidator when reasonably required to do so;
• look after and hand over to the liquidator the company's assets and records.

Creditors' Compulsory Liquidation

This generally results from a winding-up petition to the courts from an unpaid creditor who is angry and has lost patience with the debtor. The creditor is clearly serious because this step will cost around £1,500 and, if the debt is not due, costs could be awarded against them. The threat can be significant because the presentation of a winding-up petition will result in bank accounts being frozen and can be very damaging to a company's credit. The liquidator also has wide powers to enquire into the actions of directors in the period leading up to the order. The tax authorities may also decide to become a party to the petition when they become aware of it, as could other creditors, which means they would all need to be paid in full in order to halt the process.

The court must be satisfied that the company is unable to pay its debts because it:

- **has not settled a statutory demand or a letter of demand;**
- **a county court judgement has not been satisfied;**
- **it can be shown that a company's debts exceed its assets.**

The directors have several options: the company can pay the debt or oppose the petition on a number of grounds, such as disputing the debt, making a counterclaim or seeking the leave of the court to appoint an administrator instead — if this would lead to a better result for creditors. Under the protection of administration the company could then try to negotiate a CVA. Another alternative is to move quickly to put a CVA in place — without going into administration — because this automatically halts a winding-up petition.

However, once a liquidator is actually appointed, the outcome is seldom a significant realisation of value from the assets of the company, largely because it takes some time before a liquidator is appointed and begins to act. During this time, value evaporates from the business and any secured creditors will still be able to appoint receivers to sell assets.

Initially the Official Receiver (a government official) is appointed to take charge of proceedings but may be replaced at a creditors' meeting by an insolvency practitioner to act as liquidator. There is always a fear, when a government official is acting that, swamped with work, things may proceed more slowly.

Validation order

Banks will usually freeze accounts as soon as they are aware of a winding-up petition because they fear a liquidator could order them to restore monies paid out once the process has started.[12] Clearly this makes trading very difficult for the company, which can seek to have the petition overturned. However, they can also apply to the registrar or district judge for what is commonly called a validation order (though the term does not appear in the legislation) that orders the unfreezing of accounts in order to carry out specified transactions.

The directors of the company will have to appoint legal counsel and, as the company's assets are frozen, the directors will have to pay for this themselves.

The application will generally include:

- **whether the debt that gave rise to the winding-up petition is disputed and the basis of the dispute;**
- **details of the company's financial position including its assets, charges over them and liabilities;**
- **a cash and profit forecast for the period for which the order is sought;**
- **details of the payments for which an order is sought and reasons to support them;**
- **Any consents obtained from the petitioning creditor (supported by documentary evidence where appropriate).**

Where an application is made urgently to enable urgent payments (such as wages) to be made, the court may consider granting limited relief for a short period without all this evidence as long as it is satisfied that the interests of creditors are unlikely to be prejudiced.

Where the application involves a sale of property, the court will need to be satisfied that any disposal will be at its full value.

---

12 Insolvency Act 1986, S. 127 (1)(a).

The court will need to be satisfied that the company is solvent or that a particular transaction will not prejudice the interests of the unsecured creditors.

Landlords' rights in insolvency

Appointment of a liquidator or administrator stops the landlord from exercising peaceful re-entry or distraint without leave of the court. Unless a landlord holds a fixed or floating charge over the assets of the company they have three sorts of debt owed to them:

1. **unpaid rent and service charges that accrued before the formal insolvency;**
2. **rent and service charges that accrue after the point of formal insolvency;**
3. **future rent and service charges payable under the terms of the lease.**

The first and third of these will rank as an unsecured creditor in insolvency, alongside other unsecured creditors. The future rents payable may add up to put landlords amongst the biggest creditors. Some landlords will hold rent deposits, which can be utilised to pay unpaid rent accrued before the insolvency.

A liquidator, but not an administrator, can disclaim leases, rents and service charges leaving a landlord as an unsecured creditor. For an administrator who continues trading in leasehold premises, or for a liquidator who does not disclaim a lease, the rent and service charges rank as an expense of the estate and are paid in priority to the insolvency practitioner's fees and expenses, before floating charge holders, preferential and other secured creditors. If the administrator does not pay rent for use of premises then the landlord retains the right to peaceful re-entry or distraint.

CHAPTER 7
USING ADMINISTRATION TO SAVE YOUR BUSINESS

There are a number of ways in which it is possible to use the administration process to save a business from liquidation. The most common is the pre-pack.

The pre-pack

A pre-packaged (pre-pack) sale refers to an arrangement under which the sale of all or part of a company's business or assets is negotiated with a purchaser, often the directors of the company, prior to the appointment of an administrator. The sale will then be carried out almost immediately after the appointment.

This process is a response to the evidence that previous insolvency processes have had a strong tendency to destroy economic value and jobs. Very few businesses recover from them and they have primarily been a means of selling off the elements of a business. Destruction of value has meant that creditors have not had a very good deal either.

The pre-pack:

- **is very quick (after the initial planning stages) and can be done over a weekend, for example;**
- **reduces adverse publicity, with a business resuming its normal trading very quickly;**
- **reduces costs compared with other types of insolvency processes (though possibly not as much as a CVA);**

• **can enable the business to dispose of onerous contracts, branches and employees that threaten the existence of its viable parts.**

When the plan is ready and a contract of sale and purchase is drawn up, the company is quickly protected by the court while the administrator sells the business to the new owners.

This process is usually followed where commercial pressures require urgent action. As explained elsewhere in this book, the value of a company can evaporate very quickly when a business enters or even approaches bankruptcy. Customers, fearful of unreliable supply, look for new suppliers; creditors send in bailiffs, refuse to supply and petition for winding up; employees look for new jobs.

Evaporation of value

Perhaps the most striking thing is that assets miraculously lose the value they had in the company's accounts. Fixed assets such as machinery, building work carried out at business premises, fixtures and fittings etc. are shown in the balance sheet at cost, less depreciation. However, this represents a value to the business *in situ*. Once you try to move or sell that asset to a third party it becomes clear that its open market value is much lower.

Unless you sell improvements to premises to a new occupant they have no value to anyone else; whilst unless they carry on the same trade they may be of no use to them. Equipment, plant and machinery is worth less on the second-hand market, may take a long time to find a buyer, incur selling fees and often costs money to disassemble, transport and reinstall elsewhere.

Stocks of raw materials are worth less, second-hand, than was paid for them; whilst work in progress is usually of no value at all unless it is completed. Finished goods stocks are usually only worth around 30% of their book value because, in a liquidation, you discover some of them were slow sellers anyway and the cessation of the business means that the mechanism for selling them has disappeared. It is necessary to dispose of them to dealers who are wholesalers and stockholders and will sell them on eventually. This means that there are costs of stockholding as well as transportation, which explains the low valuation. Some stocks held for resale may be subject to Retention of Title claims from suppliers, which also reduce the overall value of stock.

Even debtors turn out to be worth less than their book value. Customers take advantage of the cessation of business to either not pay or, at least, to delay payment. They raise queries over invoices and deliveries, and the previous staff who dealt with these may have left. Unless the same staff are available to help with collecting debts, costs rise and recoveries fall.

There has been a great deal of adverse publicity about pre-packs where directors of a failed company put it into administration and promptly buy it out again at what is seen to be a very low price. Their new business resumes trading immediately, apparently unharmed, whilst creditors lose much if not all of their debt. Naturally this annoys the creditors. In reality the previous owners have lost their previous investment and so, whilst they can start again, they are normally not unharmed. The process has the advantage of helping to preserve businesses and jobs. It may also produce a better dividend for creditors than liquidating the business or trying to sell all or part of it as a going concern. Administrators have to explain to creditors the background to their appointment and the reasons why they considered that a 'pre-pack' sale would give the best outcome for creditors. They have to reveal the name of the purchaser of the business and the price paid, as well as details of any connection that the purchaser had with the former directors or shareholders.[13]

The government announced in early 2011 that it intends to introduce a requirement for 'administrators to give notice to creditors where they propose to sell a significant proportion of the assets of a company or its business to a connected party, in circumstances where there has been no open marketing of the assets'. This would allow creditors time to make representations

---

13 Statement of Insolvency Practice (SIP) number 16. January 2009.

to the administrator or to institute court action if they think the pre-pack or its terms are unreasonable. Newspaper reports suggest the government is considering a three day delay for all this but also that industry insiders are still trying to influence the final proposals.[14]

In order to justify a pre-pack, or any sale by the administrator to a connected party, the administrator will need a valuation of the business and its assets by a reputable, independent valuer. This may occur before the appointment of the administrator who will, nonetheless, want to be involved in choosing the valuer to ensure that it is someone they have confidence in. If the result is a low value then that may help the directors in making a bid for some or all of the assets but they cannot be certain that that will be the outcome. The directors are quite entitled to try to persuade the valuer to accept their view of value but may not succeed. The valuer's report may encourage the administrator to seek other offers for the business.

Finding an administrator

A company's accountants, solicitors or other advisers will often be able to recommend an insolvency practitioner and usually directors will have consulted advisers before reaching the decision to appoint administrators. However, if these advisers may figure amongst the creditors in an insolvency, the directors may be reluctant to let them know such an event may be looming. Administrators can also be found through the government's Insolvency Service which lists authorised practitioners and their regulating bodies: there is a search box on their website to facilitate finding an IP by area. There is also the simple expedient of an Internet search or a call to one of the accountancy bodies, who may be able to give a list of their members who are authorised insolvency practitioners in your area.

---

14 http://www.myintroducer.com/view.asp?ID=6578 [accessed 23 August 2011].

What to look for

It is then a matter of going to see the practitioner and forming a view on whether to use them. The sort of considerations will be:

- **how clearly they explain what will happen;**
- **their level of fees;**
- **how good their advice seems to be;**
- **their level of resources.**

In addition there will be intangible considerations such as how comfortable you feel with them. It may be a good idea to see more than one firm in order to compare them.

The Internet also provides the ability to conduct a search by firm, which can give some idea if people who have dealt with them have been so disgruntled as to vent their feelings. It is important to bear in mind that this will be one-sided and that the practitioner may have a different perspective.

Costs and other issues of administration

When a board of directors decides to put their company into administration they select the insolvency practitioner to perform the role but, as soon as they are appointed, the administrator is in charge. So obtain a record in advance, in writing, and in precise detail as to what has been agreed. When you agree fees, for example, make sure this includes those payable by the company prior to the appointment, when the insolvency practitioner is performing an advisory role.

The insolvency practitioner will normally ask for a sum in advance to cover their costs. For example, if you are assured that the total costs of administration will be no more than £30,000, make sure this includes the £10,000 you paid in advance: it probably doesn't. Make sure it covers expenses as well as fees. The administrator is unlikely to give a cast iron commitment over fees because they cannot be certain, in advance, what may come out of the woodwork and therefore how much work will be involved. However, you are reasonably protected if they set out their estimate and what it will cover and also what the basis of charging will be for any unanticipated work. Make sure you have charge rates for various levels of staff they may assign.

In around 60% of administrations, the secured charge holders are not repaid in full, which means that the bank is effectively paying the administrator's fees. The Office of Fair Trading has found that in the other 40% of cases — where the bank is not pressing down on fees — administration fees tend to be, on average, 9% higher.[15] It is therefore up to the appointing directors and the creditors to exert this pressure, which is not easy. On average, fees swallow 20% of the money released from administration, and another bugbear of unsecured creditors is that they often feel the administrator does not try hard enough to get the best prices once the bank has been paid off.

Suppose the appointment of an administrator is also associated with an offer from the directors or shareholders for some or all of the business. You agree the price but what is being bought may not be simple and deserves careful thought. You will generally not buy the company but will buy assets, what is included?

- **Property leases — what happens if the landlord successfully resists a transfer?**
- **Intellectual property — if the business has processes or trademarks or copyrights, are they included?**
- **Stocks — you may not want all the stocks but if you do, is there a known quantity or will there have to be a count?**
- **Debtors — the buyer will usually want to buy the debtors in order to normalise the customer relationship as soon as possible; but if not, then the administrator may want the buyer to collect the debtors — probably in return for a commission.**
- **Books and records, or at least access to them.**
- **Unprofitable parts of the business — you may be excluding parts of the business but who makes those staff redundant,**

---

15 The Market for Corporate Insolvency Practitioners, Office of Fair Trading, June 2010.

the administrator or the directors, before appointing the administrator?

What happens if there is a corporation tax or VAT recovery or part of what had been assumed to be a bad debt is recovered, or a court case the company was pursuing results in damages in favour of the company, who gets that? Or suppose the directors will continue to manage the business on behalf of the administrators for a few days — or even more — if there are profits from trading, who gets that? Don't leave these things to chance — try to cover everything. An administrator may not have the funds to continue with a court case and may seek to withdraw: do the directors want to fund its continuation in return for some or all of any damages?

The price may not be simple either. You can pay the full price on completion, or part on completion with some deferred payments. Part of the payment could be an undertaking to pay creditors, as long as this does not result in some creditors being preferred over others. The price may also be dependent on things like the value of debts recovered or the value of stocks, subject to a stock take.

The directors lose control of the process as soon as the administrators are appointed. So, if circumstances change, the administrator may be forced to reconsider any previous intentions. For example, if an alternative buyer makes a higher offer or if they discover that the previous management had been transferring assets from the business, the administrator may have to abandon their plans to sell to the previous management team.

Complaints

If creditors feel they have been disadvantaged in an administration, including where they believe the administrator has behaved improperly, they should raise their concerns formally with the insolvency practitioner who is acting. Every authorised practitioner is required to have a complaints procedure. If still dissatisfied by the results of this the remedy for an incorrect decision has to be through the courts. Although that can be an expensive process, there is a small claims procedure (covering claims of up to £15,000) through the courts that is significantly cheaper. Nonetheless, if unhappy with an insolvency practitioner's behaviour it is possible to complain through their authorising body and also to:

The Insolvency Service,
Conduct and Complaints Team Hotline,
3rd Floor, Cannon House,
18 Priory Queensway,
Birmingham
B4 6FD
Telephone: 0845 601 3546
email: enforcement.hotline@insolvency.gsi.gov.uk

Complaining is rather limited because the regulatory bodies will not intervene in particular cases. They will act if it can be shown that a member has behaved unethically and this can lead to disciplinary action. The only tough action available is through the courts.

The directors who appointed an insolvency practitioner also have rather limited recourse. As explained above, the insolvency practitioner, once appointed, acts for the creditors and not for the people who appointed them.

CHAPTER 8
IMPLICATIONS FOR DIRECTORS

If a company becomes insolvent, the legal duty of its directors changes. Instead of having a duty to the company under the Companies Act 2006, they have an over-riding duty to protect the interests of creditors under the Insolvency Act 1986.

Fraudulent preference

A company must not prefer one creditor's interests over another's — such a preference is unlawful.[16] This will most obviously arise when directors are also creditors, perhaps having not drawn all of their salary in cash, thereby leaving some as an unsecured loan. If they repay themselves before other creditors in the last two years, before the company becomes insolvent, then they are preferring one creditor — themselves — over others. The liquidator can initiate proceedings against them that may result in forced repayment, disqualification as a director or even prosecution.

The most common preferences are repayment of:

- **a bank overdraft or other secured debts to avoid personal guarantees being called in;**
- **debts to companies owned by the directors or their families.**

16 Insolvency Act 1986, S. 239-241.

But there are other acts that a liquidator can apply to the court to set aside under this heading, such as issuing security to a connected party for their pre-existing debt only after it is clear that the company is in financial difficulty.

Is there anything that a director who is not acting dishonestly can do? Sometimes it may be possible to put forward a justification for payment, although it is advisable to take legal advice. If the company is not actually insolvent or there are reasonable grounds for believing it can be saved then this may justify paying a particular creditor or repaying part of a loan in order to keep trading.

There are a number of potential consequences for directors of a company that becomes insolvent.

The year to March 2010 has seen an increase in the number of company directors facing disqualification proceedings to 2,169 (2009: 1,852) from 1,047 companies.

The law firm, *Wedlake Bell,* that compiled this data reports, 'Anecdotally, it would appear that a good many of these disqualifications are as a consequence of some directors making last ditch attempts to save their businesses or own personal financial positions but in so doing breaking the law'.[17]

Reasons for disqualification proceedings	Number to 31 March 2010
Underpaid tax	813
Accounting failures	444
Making non-commercial transactions whilst the company was insolvent	388
Fraud and theft	265
Misappropriation of assets	67

---

17 http://www.wedlakebell.org/Default.aspx?sID=1215&cID=517&ctID=43&lID=0 [accessed 23 August 2011].

(cont.)

Trading with knowledge of insolvency	40
Failure to file annual accounts	33
Phoenix companies	12
Other	107
Total	**2169**

Table: 8.1

Your credit rating will be affected immediately, and not just yours but that of anyone living at your address and particularly those sharing your surname. So if you, or immediate relatives, want to start a new business, in order to resume your career you may encounter a problem in getting a telephone line, electricity supply, credit card or bank loan. With utilities, there is unlikely to be a blanket stop on getting a connection but you will find it hard to get credit and may have to pay a deposit or pay for supplies in advance. This applies not just to directors as individuals but to companies they may set up to carry on business. Their names and addresses will appear on the particulars of the new company and will be traced back to the insolvency almost immediately.

It may seem distasteful, but an obvious way to deal with these problems is to arrange for a lifeboat before the ship founders. So, as soon as you know there is a financial problem, prepare for the worst. This may be difficult for three reasons:

1. **You are working hard to avoid insolvency. Your energy and attention is directed to this end and you have little time or inclination to focus on other things.**
2. **It is distasteful and feels grubby to be working behind the scenes to look after yourself.**
3. **There is a risk of pursuit by creditors or a liquidator if it can be shown that directors were behaving improperly.**

You have to be really careful to avoid any behaviour that is morally improper or illegal. It is essential that you take professional legal advice. Actions that are within the law but are morally questionable can alienate customers, employees, suppliers and financiers just as much as illegality. I am, however, suggesting preparing in advance because problems will arise if you do not. So, if you are a director of a business and suspect it is at risk of failure, establish a new company before that happens. Get it a bank account. It would be great if you could also get it a credit history, telephone line, and trading address but these may be difficult to achieve without breaching the duties you owe your original company.

Do not transfer assets out of the old business and into a new one unless:

- **you can demonstrate that the transaction was at market value;**
- **you can demonstrate that the transfer did not damage the trade of the old business;**
- **the shareholders of the new and old businesses are identical and have the same proportionate holding in both businesses.**

You are probably safest simply not transferring assets.

In a difficult trading situation, I considered this route to put a profitable Internet business into a new company whilst leaving the unprofitable retail business behind. I decided it was not honest and not a safe course of action. I would only have wanted to extract the profitable business because it had value in excess of what I would have paid — otherwise why do it? Expressing it like this makes it clear that the transaction would have involved taking value from the old business and therefore disadvantaging creditors.

Setting up a new business alongside the old and commencing trading in order to establish supplier accounts and a credit record is fraught with difficulty. For example, devoting time to a new business to the detriment of the old may be a breach of fiduciary duty to the old company (as well as a possible breach of your employment contract) and there is always a liquidator who might complain if value has been taken out of the old company. This process of going bust one day and starting trading again the next is referred to as a 'phoenix' because this bird from mythology was believed to die by stepping into a fire where it was consumed only to emerge reborn. It is frowned upon by banks and is often the chosen route of blatantly dishonest traders.

However... if you are an honest person you will find you are penalised for failing to take precautions.

Unfortunately I was a director of a company that we had to put into administration because of a single unprofitable site. We decided to do nothing in advance but, after applying for the administration order, we set up a new company to buy what we could from the administrators. This preserved jobs and, we thought, would ensure that most of the creditors, at least, could be paid. So we went to the suppliers and offered to pay them everything they were owed if they would continue to supply us. Well two big suppliers turned down this offer. It turned out that their credit insurers would not agree because the directors were the same as those of the failed business. They preferred to embrace the certainty of losing tens of thousands of pounds immediately rather than risk a potential loss if the resurrected business failed at some time in the future. Madness.

Lessons

> If we had established the new company earlier, opened some supplier accounts and put through a few modest orders we might have avoided this problem.

In summary, directors must take care that:

• **they devote a substantial amount of their time to oldco and not newco;**
• **there is nothing in service contracts to prevent associating with a competing company;**
• **business (to any material degree) must not be siphoned off from oldco to newco before or after insolvency: that is unmistakably fraudulent and the prison doors beckon;**
• **the intellectual or physical property of oldco must not be used to create newco;**
• **oldco's trade — particularly its customers — must not be transferred to newco (trying to buy these at fair value after the possible failure of oldco is another matter);**
• **they show that oldco had stopped trading only when there was no reasonable hope of survival — continuing would constitute wrongful trading (see below).**

Wrongful trading

Many people get into a panic about 'Trading Whilst Insolvent' and feel they must call in a liquidator immediately and cease trading. They also fear terrible personal consequences.

This is a serious matter but not one for panic. There may still be time to find a solution that may include saving some or all of the company.

Although people talk about 'Trading Whilst Insolvent' or 'Insolvent Trading' these are not offences that are defined by law. The actual legal offence is Wrongful Trading which is covered by S. 214 of the Insolvency Act 1986. So what is Wrongful Trading?

It is conduct that can only be undertaken by the director of a limited company. That status arises most obviously from being validly appointed at a meeting of the company, being entered on the company's statutory register and the appointment being notified to Companies House. However, it can also arise from being a 'shadow director' as set out in the Companies Act 2006 or a 'de facto' director as defined by common law.

A shadow director 'means a person in accordance with whose directions or instructions the directors of the company are accustomed to act'.[18]

A 'de facto' director is a person who performs the functions of a director but who has not been formally appointed as one.

Whilst it is likely to be undesirable to continue trading when you cannot pay your debts as they fall due, there may be instances where that is not improper, for example, when you have a reasonable prospect of resolving the problem quickly, such as when you believe (reasonably) that:

- **you are on the point of attracting a new investor;**
- **a profitable new order is about to be won;**
- **you believe you can reach a compromise agreement with creditors;**
- **a material asset is about to be sold.**

Any of these events might transform the circumstances of a company and enable it to pay its debts and are likely to provide a valid excuse for continuing to trade as long as the belief that the company will be able to continue is reasonably held and not reckless. The key definition is that 'before the commencement of the winding up, that person [the director of a company that goes into insolvent liquidation] knew or ought to have concluded that there was no reasonable prospect that the company would avoid going into insolvent liquidation'.[19] Insolvent liquidation occurs

18 Companies Act 2006, S. 251(1).
19 The Insolvency Act 1986, S. 214(2)(b).

when 'a company goes into liquidation at a time when its assets are insufficient for the payment of its debts and other liabilities and for the expenses of winding up'.[20] Furthermore, that that person fails to 'take every step with a view to minimising the loss to the company's creditors as he ought to have taken'.[21]

But what are the 'facts that a director ought to know or ascertain, the conclusions which they ought to reach and the steps which they ought to take'? Is this not a matter of guesswork? They are judged by the criteria of 'a reasonably diligent person having both:

- **the general knowledge, skill and experience that may reasonably be expected of a person carrying out the same functions as are carried out by that director, in relation to the company;**
- **the general knowledge and skills that that director has'.[22]**

So a marketing director, for example, will be expected to have known or done what a reasonably competent and diligent director should have known or done in the circumstances. But if that particular director possessed an accountancy qualification then they will be judged by a stricter criterion of what a reasonably competent and diligent director who has an accountancy qualification should have known or done.

If a director has been dishonest, negligent, reckless or simply failed to act as a reasonable person would, then there are significant penalties for wrongful trading:[23]

- **any director can be required to contribute any sum 'to the company's assets as the court thinks proper'.**
- **any director may be referred to the Secretary of State, which could result in disqualification from acting as a director under the Directors Disqualification Act 1986.**

---

20 The Insolvency Act, S. 214(6).
21 *Ibid.*
22 Insolvency Act 1986, S. 214(4).
23 Insolvency Act 1986, S. 214–218.

As the table above shows, directors' disqualifications as a result of wrongful trading on its own are comparatively rare, with most resulting from acts of misconduct or dishonesty of one form or another.

Personal guarantees

Directors are often asked to give personal guarantees by their bankers and sometimes by landlords and even other creditors. This removes the protection that is meant to be provided by the limited company structure. It is often unavoidable but it is not always unavoidable. I was a director of a company for over ten years where we refused to give personal guarantees and the bank agreed to our terms; so it can be done. Remember that you are in a negotiation and see what you can achieve. If you concede the guarantee, try to avoid giving a fixed charge on your home. For example, do you have other property assets or investments that they would agree to have as security instead of your home?

In the event of business insolvency, your personal guarantee may be called upon and you can lose your house or even become personally bankrupt. Before allowing this to happen, consider whether there is a viable alternative that can be negotiated with the bank. It may be possible to repay the debt over a period of years instead of selling the house. Talk to them. On the other hand, rather than committing to an impossible burden for many years, it may be preferable to accept the personal bankruptcy option.

Personal bankruptcy

Personal bankruptcy means you cannot be a company director, a shadow director or be concerned in the management of a company. It is an offence for an officer of a company to act on instructions from an individual who is an undischarged bankrupt. This is designed to prevent a bankrupt from getting around the law by effectively acting as a director through the agency of another person.

Bank accounts are frozen. A bankrupt has difficulty borrowing and must declare they are a bankrupt if borrowing £500 or more.

They usually cannot have personal credit cards. A bankrupt's credit rating is adversely affected long after they are discharged. The bankruptcy is not expunged from credit records for six years.

The valuable assets of a bankrupt will be sold to repay debts. This does not apply to basic belongings needed for home life but will apply to anything of value.

The bankruptcy is normally discharged after one year but a share of income can be taken for up to three years to repay creditors. However, bankruptcy restrictions can be extended for as long as 15 years if the bankruptcy resulted from reckless or dishonest behaviour.

Personal liability

This is dealt with in various sections of this book but there are many circumstances following insolvency where a company director may be personally liable and are summarised below;

Fraudulent trading

If, in the course of winding up a company, it appears that business has been carried on with an intent to defraud, the liquidator can apply to the courts for 'any persons who were knowingly parties... to make such contributions... as the court thinks proper'.[24] This is in addition to any criminal penalties for fraud[25] and an individual may also be banned from serving as a director of a company.[26]

Wrongful trading

A report is made by a liquidator or the Official Receiver to the courts and/or to the Secretary of State if one or more of the directors should have concluded there was no reasonable prospect of avoiding insolvent liquidation. See 'Wrongful Trading' above.

---

24 Insolvency Act 1986, S. 213.
25 ibid S. 215.
26 Directors Disqualification Act 1986, S. 4.

Personal liability for business taxes

There are circumstances in which company directors can be liable as individuals for unpaid taxes of a business that becomes insolvent.

Directors can become personally liable for the 'wilful failure' of their company to operate PAYE on their remuneration. (Under S. 71 of The Criminal Justice Act 1988 (Confiscation Orders 1996) and S. 114 The Social Security and Administration Act 1992.)

When a company fails to pay over PAYE and NI contributions the Crown has the right to consider an action against the directors personally, under S. 121C of the Social Security Administration Act 1992. This seems to be rarely used but it is there!

Directors can be liable if there has been any persistent failure to pay over PAYE/NIC when other payments are being made on time; if directors' remuneration has continued to be paid during the period; if the individual has been involved with other companies which have failed to pay over taxes; and if the company has been using the Crown as a bank.

Finally, where the directors of a company which has failed owing substantial amounts of tax, PAYE/NIC or VAT, are involved in a new business, the tax authorities are also increasingly making use of their powers to demand that the new business pays a deposit to cover tax that may fall due in future. The amount required can be the equivalent of a full year's worth of expected tax for the new business. While the deposit, less what turns out to be due, will be returned at the end of a year, it can obviously be a substantial sum to find for a new start-up, but do not ever be tempted to carry on trading without paying it as this can lead to criminal proceedings.

Directors' loan accounts

There are risks to directors' loans or an overdrawn current account. Directors often pay themselves partly through taking loans from the business and then repaying them in due course from the proceeds of dividends. This may save tax but it carries a risk if the business gets into financial difficulties because if it becomes insolvent then that loan will be called in by the administrator or liquidator.

Disqualification

The Company Directors Disqualification Act 1986 applies to directors of companies that have gone into liquidation. The process can be quite slow.

> MG Rover collapsed in 2005 with the loss of 6,000 jobs and debts of £1.3bn. An independent report found the Phoenix Four — Peter Beale, John Towers, Nick Stephenson, and John Edwards — manipulated MG Rover's assets and income streams, such as land and its financing arm, through the creation of companies in which they, rather than the creditors of MG Rover, had an interest.[27]
>
> However, they were not disqualified until 2011, nearly six years after the insolvency.

Disqualification can result in a ban from serving as a company director or from being involved in the management of a business of between two and fifteen years, with the more severe penalties reserved for repeat offenders, dishonesty or fraud. Steven Law, president of R3, the association of business recovery professionals, was quoted as saying that the number of individuals disqualified in 2009 was 1,387. The same article reports that the UK government is seeking to save money from the insolvency service budget, which may reduce the number of disqualifications and, indeed, has already resulted in a substantial drop from 1,594 in 2002.[28] Over the same period between 2002 and 2009 the number of directors reported to the Insolvency Service for alleged

---

27 Ruddick, Graham 'MG Rover's "Phoenix Four" banned from being directors', *The Daily Telegraph*, 9 May 2011.
28 'Shady bosses given licence to operate despite warnings', Alex Spence, *The Times*, 28 December 2010.

misconduct by insolvency practitioners rose from 3,539 to 7,030. However, even if the probability of suffering disqualification has fallen, the consequences can be serious with even a short ban likely to affect the availability of credit or of directors' insurance.

The key points on which the Department of Business, Industry and Skills seeks to ban directors on are:

- **failure to submit annual accounts to Companies House on time;**
- **failure to submit annual returns to Companies House on time;**
- **excessive salaries or drawings when the company was plainly insolvent;**
- **continuing to trade when he or she knew the company was insolvent (trading whilst knowingly insolvent);**
- **continuing to take credit when there was 'no reasonable prospect' of creditors being paid;**
- **misrepresentation of facts about the company;**
- **failure to respond or comply with a liquidator's requests.**

If disqualified, a director may not act as a director or manager in the disqualification period; doing so constitutes a criminal offence and penalties can include imprisonment for up to two years or a fine (or both).

Remember that if a director or manager acts on the instructions of a person who has been disqualified, they too may be made personally liable for the company debts. So beware of banned directors.

Corporate governance

Corporate governance describes the systems, procedures and behaviours by which a company organises itself. It is particularly important at times of severe stress when poor governance can lead to bad decisions.

The phrase 'financial distress' speaks for itself. This is a difficult time for directors of the company. There are personal worries about what happens to guarantees that have been given to the bank, what the future holds and how to earn a living. These concerns are often mixed up with the effects on family, with stress on relationships resulting from lack of income, the lost value of an investment in the business and loss of self-esteem. One feels a failure. It is embarrassing to admit failure to family, friends and acquaintances. There is all that hard work that has been invested in the business, perhaps over years: will it all be for nothing? There are also concerns about responsibilities to staff who may have worked for the business for a long time and may lose their jobs and possibly pension entitlements.

This burden of distress will often become a governance issue because directors can be reluctant to face up to reality and because it can prompt avoidance behaviour that may be improper or even unlawful. It is also a governance issue because strains will inevitably appear between the different partners in a business that is in trouble — with shareholders and directors taking different views. They may have different interests but, regardless of this, there is a tendency to believe there is fault and that more of it lies with others than with oneself. So there will be disagreements about what to do and how to do it.

When a company is in financial difficulty, it is more important than ever that those in charge work together as an effective team if there is to be any chance of saving the business. At the same time, change may be necessary. Goals and strategies may need to be revised, reorganisation may be necessary and some of the top team may need to leave. In either case, governance procedures are important.

The board must work as a team to agree what has gone wrong and what to do. Often the board members are aware of some of the difficult decisions that are necessary. If they were easy they would have been taken before. Decisions must be taken. These may involve sacking close friends or even family. They may involve abandoning key suppliers, or projects or parts of the business, despite emotional ties.

Non-executive directors can be valuable at times like this if they are independent. Independence is not just a lack of formal ties to the business but is an attitude of mind. They may have a broader perspective and be able to take a more dispassionate view, with less emotion invested in the decisions that need to be taken. Their opinions should be sought by the other directors.

Protecting yourself

A completely different aspect of governance that is important in stressful times is following proper procedures. If a business does fail, the actions of its directors and senior executives in the two years prior to the event come under scrutiny by an administrator and then by a liquidator. Sales of property are examined to ensure they were not carried out at an undervaluation or to connected parties; possible trading whilst insolvent and wrongful trading are investigated. Preference of one creditor over another is considered. Decisions that may have been reckless or incompetent are looked into. The repercussions of any of these may be considerable with individuals potentially incurring personal liability, disqualification as a director or criminal charges.

The honest director or executive should ensure there is a clear record of how, when and why decisions were taken in the run-up to a company failure. Of course you may not know that bankruptcy is around the corner — though, often, financial distress shows itself quite some time before a failure — and this is an argument for always keeping proper records as a matter of course. Particularly if a company is in financial difficulties it is important to hold regular and frequent management and board meetings, as well as minuting the discussions and decisions taken and filing these carefully. Merely continuing a practice, say, of holding quarterly board meetings, does not demonstrate careful management or taking the situation seriously. Depending upon circumstances, management meetings may be held weekly or even daily in a crisis. Management accounts should be prepared regularly, even in a crisis, both to help evaluate and manage the situation and also to document this. Failure to produce accounts may be taken to indicate recklessness or neglect.

Whilst the law requires minutes to be kept of board meetings for six years, it does not specify how they should be written up nor does it say anything about other executive meetings. Comprehensive minutes should be taken of meetings where decisions are made, not only to record what they were, but also that they were made after careful consideration. This is good management practice anyway. When records are not made people inevitably interpret the outcome of meetings in the light of what they wanted to happen. There are disagreements about what was decided and different people implement different (and incompatible) interpretations. Therefore, either ensure there are formal minutes or confirm what happened by circulating a brief memo to those present or concerned in the meeting's outcome. At a minimum this should say who was present, when and where it was held, should detail the decision and also any special circumstances or conditions. If the decision could be contentious, state briefly why the decision was taken.

CHAPTER 9
STARTING AGAIN

Before starting again, it's essential that you analyse what went wrong last time. Preparing a plan to do exactly the same again is unlikely to get support from investors, bankers and suppliers and — worse — it is unlikely to succeed. So produce a plan (see Chapter 3) that highlights:

- **what went wrong and why it went wrong;**
- **what you have learnt;**
- **what you are proposing to do differently.**

Above all, it is important to establish and rebuild trust. It is therefore important to be open and transparent and not to hide what happened.

Getting a bank account

Banks are very reluctant to open a new account for a company run by an individual whose company has just failed. This appears to result partly from bad publicity attracted to 'phoenix companies', partly from some sort of moral view and possibly from a feeling that there is a greater banking risk in such cases. However, my experience of difficulty obtaining a bank account related to a company that was not going to use overdraft or loan facilities, so it is hard to see how risk could have been a factor. A significant issue in the decision appears to be whether the bankers for the previous business lost money in the liquidation. Nonetheless, if you are persistent and try different banks, and even different branches (ensure they are not within one area because the same senior manager may review applications from different branches), it is likely that one or more banks will eventually provide facilities, as we found.

Obtaining an overdraft is likely to be more difficult and will certainly require personal guarantees from directors. One of the problems with personal guarantees is that they are demanded from all directors, even those not actively concerned in the running of a business. This may prove a problem if a non-active director refuses to give a guarantee.

Bear in mind that bank services such as BACS[29] count as borrowing. This proved problematic for paying our monthly wages through BACS and we had to pay by online banking transfers instead, which was inconvenient but got around the problem.

Utilities

Utility companies seem to take less of a moral stance than banks, but to be more risk averse. Even more than is the case with a bank, it is impossible to do business without utilities such as electricity, telephone and the postal service. The utilities companies are required, as monopolies, to provide a basic service to anyone, but they can and do impose conditions — such as a security deposit, which can tie up scarce capital.

Suppliers

Suppliers may not be willing to deal again with individuals whose previous business became insolvent, owing them money. But if the manufacturer won't supply you, maybe there is a wholesaler (who didn't lose money) who will. If the manufacturer will open a new account, they may not offer the same credit limit or even the

---

29 Bankers Automated Clearing Services (BACS) is a UK scheme for electronic processing of financial transactions. It is often used by companies, amongst other things, for paying staff wages.

same prices that your previous business enjoyed. These matters are entirely a matter of negotiation and will depend upon the individuals involved, and the degree to which they feel you were culpable. When planning for the new business be cautious, and assume worse prices and shorter credit periods in your forecasts.

If it is proving difficult to open accounts, it will usually be worthwhile to visit the supplier carrying a business plan for the new business. Try to persuade them. As a last ditch fallback, if a supplier is critical to the new venture, is it possible to offer to repay them what they lost in the insolvency, even if spread over several years? Clearly this would be dependent upon them offering suitable credit terms and pricing.

CHAPTER 10
PRACTICAL STEPS FOR INVESTORS, CREDITORS AND EMPLOYEES

Many people lose when a company gets into financial difficulties. Jobs, pensions, savings, the dignity of going to work can all be lost. It is often a devastating experience but there are sometimes steps that can be taken to mitigate the loss. These almost invariably depend on being close to the action and knowing what is going on.

Shareholders
What is a shareholder's liability in insolvency?

It seems worthwhile to summarise quickly what a shareholder is because the simple idea can get complicated. The capital of a limited company is divided into shares of equal value owned by shareholders (also called members of the company). In the event of business failure, they are liable only for the money they have invested already. Unlike a partnership or sole trader, they can't be called upon to make good the money the business can't pay its creditors, unless they are also directors and, in that capacity, are found guilty of wrongful trading.

Some companies issue 'partly paid' shares. The original shareholders will only have paid the company some of the face value of the shares and, in the event of a failure, they or anyone who has acquired the shares will be personally liable for the balance. Most shares are 'fully paid'. Some companies, particularly not-for-profit ones may be 'companies limited by guarantee', where the shareholders have provided a guarantee to pay in money if necessary but this is a purely nominal amount.

What can be done?

Insolvency usually means that shareholders lose their entire investment but there are cases where something can be salvaged. The options include:

- **buy the business out of administration;**
- **invest further money to support the business;**
- **provide support and advice to management;**
- **replace the management team;**
- **investigate the conduct of directors.**

Clearly shareholders can support a sale of part of the business as a going concern, either through administration or through a CVA. If that is the case, the shareholders themselves may want to be involved in the purchase, either together with or separately from any plan pursued by the directors. They may also be prepared to provide further funding to support the business.

Shareholders are in a much stronger position if they know what is going on and therefore can apply pressure. It is therefore a sensible strategy for shareholders of a company in financial distress to meet the directors and to be briefed on the situation. Although there is a risk of being embroiled as a 'shadow director', and potentially incurring liabilities, this risk is small if the shareholders do not become involved in day-to-day management and do not give instructions to staff. The ability of shareholders to obtain information and to exert influence on strategy clearly depends upon personal relationships but also on their share of the votes.

It must not be forgotten that the company's shareholders can replace the directors. They may be reluctant to do this in the midst of a crisis, when this action may leave the business rudderless at a critical time. But, on the other hand, if the directors are floundering and don't know what to do, or are pursuing misguided policies, then other individuals, particularly someone experienced in turnaround's, may have a better prospect of saving the business.

Shareholders can remove or appoint a director through an ordinary resolution, requiring a simple majority, at a meeting. Shareholders representing 10% or more of the voting capital can require the company to call a meeting and to circulate a resolution to members.[30] Special notice is required of the resolution and the company must receive notification of an intention to put it forward at least 28 days before the meeting.[31] The director may be entitled to compensation under their service agreement and is entitled to protest against removal by requiring the company to distribute representations to shareholders before the meeting.[32] Shareholders who want to pursue such a course of action should take legal advice. If there is a clear majority of the votes in favour of removal or replacement of directors then a negotiated agreement might achieve the change faster and with less disruption to the business.

Shareholders can press the administrator or liquidator to investigate the actions of directors in the run-up to insolvency. If it turns out that any transactions can be challenged then it may be possible to overturn them or to make the directors personally liable for some or all of the debts of the company, which might increase the sums available for creditors and shareholders. However, the influence of the shareholder is restricted since the administrator or liquidator is primarily responsible to the creditors. It may be a matter of deploying 'soft' influencing skills. Nonetheless, there is a legal requirement on an administrator or liquidator to look into the conduct of people who have been directors of an insolvent company in the three years prior to the insolvency and to send a report to the authorities and to highlight any concerns. The sort of issues occurring prior to the insolvency, that a shareholder in a private company might become aware of could include:

---

30 Companies Act 2006, S. 303
31 Companies Act 2006, S. 168.
32 Companies Act 2006, S .169.

- **transfer of assets out of the business (perhaps at an undervaluation);**
- **transactions with connected parties;**
- **excessive payments to directors or staff.**

The losses incurred by shareholders may be partly recovered through the tax system. Business losses can be offset against either capital gains or against taxable income in the year. If an Enterprise Investment Scheme was used to finance an investment then there is an automatic right to offset losses against either capital gains or income tax. Any UK taxpayer can make a 'negligible value claim' through their tax return or can write to HMRC at any time to make it. The claim establishes their capital loss but they can opt for this to be offset against income tax instead. There can be complexities to these reliefs, with investments in businesses such as share traders ineligible, very large investments and some types of preference shares excluded etc. But the procedure is straightforward in the majority of cases and HMRC provides a helpsheet that explains the relief (http://www.hmrc.gov.uk/helpsheets/hs286.pdf [accessed 23 August 2011). Losses can usually be carried back to the previous tax year, which speeds up the recovery and can also be worth more for investors who were higher rate taxpayers in the previous year but not in the current year.

Correspondence from the administrator or liquidator should be sufficient to establish the loss in value that is being claimed.

Creditors — what to do

The starting point for creditors is before a customer becomes insolvent and should be part of a good debtor management system.

1. **Take full details of a new customer, including business address and head/registered office address (if different) and how long they have been at these addresses. Take the full names of directors if it is a limited company.**

2. Take up references when you start dealing with a new customer. Check whether they normally pay on time. If the prospective order is a large one make sure the customer gives you substantial references. Telephone the referee.

3. Check whether they have had county court judgements against them (see http://www.trustonline.org.uk).

4. To support a large order, ask for their latest three years' accounts. This allows you to spot any trends, such as falling sales and profits or increasing borrowing or creditors rising as a percentage of sales. Do not be fobbed off with abbreviated accounts (this is what all smaller companies are required to file: they will have a set of the full accounts too).

5. Companies House provides an inexpensive monitoring service on companies that will alert you to sudden changes.

6. Google new or substantial debtors and their directors from time to time. You never know what may pop up. If there Is a pattern of directors being associated with failed companies then take note.

7. For larger amounts of credit consider using a credit reference agency (see below) or set up a subscription that provides a check for all new customers.

8. You may want to think about credit insurance if the failure of a customer might endanger your company.

9. Set a credit limit for each customer and stick to it.

10. Use an accounting package that warns you when an invoice is overdue for payment or when a credit limit is exceeded. Record late payments so you can see if this is a habit and if it is getting worse.

11. Act quickly. If this is a first time payment that has been late, and it is for a relatively small amount, then you may want to allow them up to a week. If it is not the first time you may want to call before the payment is due and ask when you will be paid.

12. Speak to the customer and ask why payment is late — some common excuses are shown below. Be firm.

13. Be prepared to withhold supplies to the customer.
14. Remember that a good customer, who does not pay, is not a good customer.
15. Be supportive of a good customer who explains a problem in advance and who convinces you the problem is short-term *but* remember that if they become insolvent you need to be one of the early, aggressive creditors who gets paid out before that happens, and not one of the over-polite, slow-moving ones who lose everything.

Detailed actions

- If an invoice is overdue, send a statement.
- If this does not get you anywhere and telephone calls don't work, send a Final Warning Letter that is dated and states that you will commence legal action if you do not receive payment within seven days.
- Before taking legal action, speak to someone in authority in order to:
  - persuade them you are serious and get them to pay;
  - gauge whether they are able to pay;
  - negotiate partial payment on account or a schedule of payments etc.
- Obtain a County Court Summons form from your local court, complete it and send a copy to the customer — reiterating your demand but giving them another few days — perhaps just two or three.
- Issue the summons to the court. You will have to pay a fee at this stage. Assuming it is unopposed, judgement may be granted after 14 days. Call the debtor, tell them of the judgement and ask again for payment, telling them they have 28 days before the judgement is registered and available to credit reference agencies.
- Proceed with obtaining a warrant of execution — an instruction to the court to collect the money, using a bailiff to seize goods to hold for sale, to pay the sum due plus expenses.

- If that does not work because of difficulties finding assets to seize, consider a winding-up petition — this is more expensive and using it must depend upon whether you believe the debtor has sufficient assets to be sold to pay your debt.

Excuses for late payment

There are common excuses used by even the biggest companies. Some of them are true, sometimes the person you are dealing with can't be bothered, sometimes they are just delaying tactics and the company is in financial difficulties. It is never in your interests to antagonise the person you are speaking to, however cross you are and however unpleasant they are. Always be polite. Never be brusque, sarcastic or raise your voice.

'We don't have your invoice on the system: please send a copy.'

Take the name and position of the person you are speaking to. Send a copy, then call back and speak to the same person again and ask when payment will be made.

'Sorry, our system is down.'

Ask how often this happens and how long it will last. Call back a little later and see if they are up again. Ask to speak to someone more senior. Ask for a manual payment by cheque or bank transfer, on account, even if not for the full amount.

'The cheque is in the post.'

Ask where, when and by whom was it posted and what class of stamp was used. Call back one or two days later if it has still not arrived and ask to speak to someone more senior. Escalate pressure.

'We are waiting for a large payment.'

A difficult one and much depends upon your relationship with the customer and whether you believe them. If you are owed a substantial sum, and are concerned, ask for a contact with this third party in order to check the story.

'We have a cash-flow problem.'

The company may be insolvent. Again much will depend upon your relationship with the customer and whether you believe they will survive. This is often a signal for using all the haste and pressure you can, to get paid before they become insolvent. You may want to insist on payment, asking if they are engaged in wrongful trading, or threatening to go down the route that will lead to a winding-up petition. It is not your concern whether paying you might be a fraudulent preference. Even if a liquidator appointed in future may be able to recover some money from you, you must be in a stronger negotiating position if you have the money now.

'The cheque signatory is away/you will have to wait for next month's cheque run.'

There must be a system to make essential payments, such as one to stop a County Court Judgement. Speak to someone in authority and obtain commitment to pay you too — even something on account.

Bouncing cheques

An extreme form of an excuse is a cheque or direct debit that is not honoured. This may arise from either the debtor instructing their bank not to pay, or there being no money in the account. This opens the opportunity to sue on the cheque rather than the debt. Many people don't realise that someone who receives a cheque that bounces can sue for the cheque rather than the debt itself. There are very limited legal defences for cancelling payment, essentially only that goods were not supplied or the transaction was fraudulent. So a legal action may quickly and cheaply result in a county court judgement.

Of course this does not help payment if the debtor has no money but either the summons or the CCJ itself may assist negotiations.

Debt recovery agencies

These private companies have no rights to force entry or seize goods. They will try to recover debts by telephoning, writing letters and visiting premises. Companies that pursue debts regulated by the Consumer Credit Act must be licensed and comply with the Office of Fair Trading (OFT) guidance code. The OFT may take action against agencies or those they act for if they engage in unfair practices, which may include:

- **using stationery or logos etc. that suggest they have court authority or official status;**
- **falsely claiming that legal action has been taken when it has not;**
- **employing harassment or threats;**
- **threatening third party disclosure unless legally entitled to;**
- **failure to leave premises when asked.**

Solicitor's letter

A solicitor's letter is really only a way of turning up the heat and showing you are serious. It is another threat. However, it also costs money to get issued and does not actually amount to action other than a threat to do something.

County court claim

Before going to court look at other options to recover a debt and consider whether it is worthwhile. Consider:

- **whether the debtor has a reasonable argument for not paying;**
- **whether you can prove the debt exists;**
- **the time and expense involved in proceedings;**
- **whether the debtor is able to pay.**

Above all, there is no point in using the courts if the debtor can't pay. Therefore check whether they already have outstanding county court judgements; perhaps check their credit ratings with agencies. If they probably can't pay then look at other methods of extracting payment — perhaps for a lesser amount or over a period of time or getting goods that have been supplied returned.

To start proceedings get a form from your local county court or apply online at http://www.moneyclaim.gov.uk [accessed 23 August 2011]. After registering the claim the court sends it to the debtor who has 14 days to reply. There are three possible outcomes:

1. **No response, in which case the creditor asks for immediate judgement.**
2. **The debtor admits the debt and either:**
   a. **makes an offer to pay that is accepted;**
   b. **makes no offer or an unacceptable one.**
3. **The debtor acknowledges service but disputes the debt.**

In case 2b, the court may issue a decision without a hearing but case 3 is likely to result in a hearing. The way this is dealt with will depend upon the size of the claim.

Small claims	Under £5,000
Fast track	£5,000 to £25,000
Multi-track	Over £25,000 or more complex claims

Enforcement

Having obtained judgement reconsider the debtor's circumstances, because enforcement will cost more money, which is only recoverable if the debtor is able to pay.

• **You can ask the court for an 'order to obtain information from the judgement debtor'.**
• **You can try negotiating with the debtor again.**
• **You can apply for a petition to wind up the company but this may prove more expensive and, if the company is insolvent, there may be no funds to pay unsecured creditors. This step is often taken when creditors are simply angry with the debtor or believe their debtor may be trying to move assets out of reach.**

- Apply for a warrant of execution. This asks the court officials to send in bailiffs who will enter premises, seize goods and sell them to cover the amount of the CCJ and the costs of the enforcement. Action through a county court can recover amounts between £600 and £5,000. For larger amounts it will be necessary to seek enforcement through the high court which is more complex and expensive and may require the help of a solicitor.
- It is also possible to apply through the court for a Garnishee Order (or Third Party Debt Order) that is served on someone who owes your debtor money, such as a bank (who holds a deposit from them) or a customer. This order, that depends on you knowing who holds money due to your debtor, requires them to pay it directly to you.
- You can apply for a charging order, which places a charge against property owned by the debtor. This is like a mortgage and can prevent the debtor from selling property or can be used to force its sale. The process can be complex and the debtor has a number of grounds on which it can oppose the grant of such an order.

Debtors and county court claims

Having received a summons a debtor has 14 days to respond. Options at this stage are:

- ask for another 14 days to respond;
- admit the claim but seek time to pay;
- defend the claim.

A County Court Judgement appears on an official register where it will be seen by credit rating agencies and will affect the ability of a business to obtain credit or raise loans. It also, as explained above, opens further avenues for a creditor to recover their debt. There are limited means to remove a record of a CCJ from the register. It expires and is removed after six years or it is not registered if it is satisfied within 28 days of being issued. The only other way is to apply to the court on grounds such as not having received proper notice of the action, or legal error, or a mistake in the register. Legal advice should be taken. The government website warns against 'credit repair companies' that claim to be able to remove CCJs from the register.

The statutory demand

This is a cheap way to recover a debt whilst increasing the level of threat. You can write the letter yourself or download a sample letter 4.1 at http://www.insolvency.gov.uk/forms/ englandwalesforms.htm [accessed 23 August 2011].

It must tell the corporate debtor:

• **how much must be paid;**
• **when payment must be made — for example, immediately or by a certain date;**
• **what will happen if the demand is ignored — for example, court action to recover the debt;**
• **details of who they can contact about the demand;**
• **their right to dispute the demand.**

The debtor has 21 days to satisfy the demand or 18 days to challenge it in court to get it cancelled. If neither of these things is done, the creditor can apply to the court after 21 days for the company to be wound up. However, this is when the procedure gets more expensive as court fees become payable. The demand can be a very effective threat when a debtor can pay, has no reasonable excuse, but is not willing to pay. The winding-up petition will have to be registered and can affect the credit rating of even the largest company. In fact, the issue of a winding-up petition may create an automatic breach of bank covenants by your debtor, so their embarrassment can be considerable. In practical terms, I have found even the threat of a statutory demand a very effective way of clearing up old debts.

However... the courts have become resistant to the over-use of this technique when a debtor company is clearly not insolvent and other means of extracting payment have not been tried.

What a debtor should do about a statutory demand

To prevent a statutory demand escalating to a winding-up petition, the following steps are necessary.

- **Pay the debt that is demanded.**
- **Reduce the amount owed below £750 (this is the minimum amount that can result in a bankruptcy order).**
- **Offer some form of settlement to the creditor. This may include a schedule of payments or some form of legal security that will satisfy them that they will be paid in due course.**
- **If you have a good reason why you should not pay, apply to the courts to have the demand set aside. Forms 6.4 and 6.5 are available from the government's insolvency website and list some of the grounds for set-aside.**
- **Look for technical failings. If the demand fails to give the name and contact for a person you can speak to about it (either the creditor or their agent) or if they will not put you through to a person, the demand may be invalid. Always try ringing to see if you can speak to the person responsible.**

Where there is a dispute in relation to a debt, the debtor company can apply to the court for an injunction restraining the creditor from presenting a winding-up petition. In such cases, where the debtor and creditor companies want to avoid the costs involved in a court case, other methods for resolving the dispute should be considered, such as arbitration, mediation and Alternative Dispute Resolution (ADR). ADR includes arbitration but also conciliation and mediation schemes: it is often provided by a supplier's trade association and may be offered through that supplier's terms and conditions. These schemes are often nonbinding and still leave the customer free to take legal action if unhappy with the outcome.[33]

Interest on late payment

The Late Payment of Commercial Debts (Interest) Act 1998 gives all businesses the right to claim interest on late payments of commercial debt. It may be useful to increase a claim against a debtor that is insolvent if there is a reasonable chance of recovering the money. It may also be used to increase pressure on a debtor who does not pay since it runs at the reference rate (usually the bank rate) plus 8%. Amendments in 2002 also give the claimant the right to compensation for reasonable debt recovery costs and to challenge customers' use of unfair contract terms that seek to limit rights to interest or compensation.

Solvent businesses sometimes meet such a claim by refusing to deal further with the supplier or by paying the basic debt but refusing to pay the interest claim. It is then up to the creditor to seek a county court judgement for the unpaid interest.

Recovering money from an insolvent company

The first signs that a trade creditor will pick up about a customer becoming insolvent may be that telephone calls are not answered, and that premises are closed (perhaps with a sign on the window referring callers to an administrator or liquidator). As soon as a creditor becomes aware that the company has become insolvent or is going through a process of solvent liquidation, they should make contact with the administrator or liquidator to notify a claim and make sure they are not missed. Companies House maintains a register of companies going through insolvency and will be able to give details of the administrator or liquidator.

The Official Receiver or an insolvency practitioner will try to contact all creditors they are aware of within three months of appointment. They will ask for a statement of the claim which

---

33 http://www.adviceguide.org.uk/c_alternative_dispute_resolution.pdf [accessed 23 August 2011].

will specify what it is for and the date it became payable. It can be confusing but the phrase used is to 'prove a claim' yet you probably don't need to provide proof at this stage. The term really only means to make your claim, usually required in writing. Further documentation such as invoices or proof of delivery may be required at a later stage but, in most cases, your claim will only be checked against company records and accepted.

If there is a retention of title clause in the terms and conditions of trade, the creditor should act immediately to notify this claim and to demand that their goods are kept segregated and not disposed of. They should arrange with the insolvency practitioner to send representatives to physically attend the premises as soon as possible to try to identify the goods. It is unlikely that they will be released straight away because the insolvency practitioner will examine the claim, but being able to enter premises to identify, segregate and even label the goods will improve chances of success — so press to be allowed to do so.

If a creditor's claim is disputed then recourse is to the courts. The administrator or liquidator has to give reasons for the rejection.

There are various ways of finding who is dealing with a case.

- **Start by calling the premises and asking what is happening.**
- **The *London Gazette* website publishes insolvency notices.**
- **Use the Companies House WebCheck service.**
- **Contact the insolvency service enquiry line (0845 602 9848).**

It can take weeks, months or even years to realise assets. The individual handling the case should be chased from time to time to check progress. Creditors will be sent a 'report to creditors' which will give information about the assets and liabilities of the company or individual, and the circumstances of the insolvency. They will be notified automatically if any money is available for distribution to unsecured creditors.

It is important to read this report carefully. If you are a creditor and believe the company or its directors have withheld information about assets or may have transferred them out of the business, you should write to the Official Receiver about them, quoting the company name and number (correspondence from the company as well as details of it at Companies House will give the company number). Be careful not to make wild allegations that cannot be proved and which may amount to slander. Use measured and temperate language but describe your suspicions and any supporting evidence.

Creditors' meetings

There are various routes to a creditors' meeting.

If a winding-up order has been obtained, the Official Receiver acts in the first instance and decides whether there are sufficient assets available to attract an insolvency practitioner. If so then creditors are notified of a creditors' meeting to appoint a liquidator. If creditors representing 25% of total debts insist on a meeting then they have to notify the Official Receiver in writing and lodge a deposit to cover costs.

If a CVA is to be agreed then a creditors' meeting must be called by the nominee to approve it. An administrator will usually call a meeting of creditors unless there will be no value to distribute to unsecured creditors, or unless the company is solvent and will pay its debts in due course. For a Creditors' Voluntary Liquidation, the company directors will call a creditors' meeting.

Further meetings of creditors may be called if demanded by creditors holding at least 25% by value of unsecured debts. They may also be called by the insolvency practitioner to get guidance from creditors. Submit a Proof of Debt form and also, if attending the meeting, a completed proxy form to authorise the individual to vote on behalf of a company.

Order of priority for repayment of creditors

Secured creditors are paid first when a debtor's assets are realised. In an administration, for example, they may have given up their right to appoint their own administrator or receiver but, in return, the administrator appointed by the company or creditors will have agreed to pay them first from the proceeds.

If they have enforced their right to appoint their own person then, after the sale, any surplus money is then handed over to the trustee or liquidator. This is then distributed as follows:

- **Liquidation fees and charges — this does not include court fees.**
- **Preferential creditors — including wages owed from the four months before the date of the insolvency order, up to a maximum of £800, as well as all holiday pay and contributions to occupational pension schemes.**
- **Any creditor holding a floating charge over an asset, such as a debenture.**
- **Unsecured creditors.**
- **Interest payable on debts.**
- **Shareholders.**

The liquidator or administrator must give details of payments to each creditor, if asked, but can charge for this.

Tracing a creditor

If a creditor's telephone number is unavailable or if letters are returned marked 'gone away' it is important to act at once:

- **Check with the local Royal Mail Sorting Office to see whether the customer is still at the address or whether there is a forwarding address.**
- **If practical, send someone round to the premises to check if the customer is still there or whether neighbours have an alternative address. Make sure that confidential information about the customer and their debt is not divulged.**
- **If you know other suppliers ask them if they have an address for the business.**
- **Check with Companies House to see if the business is on their list of insolvent companies.**
- **Contact the company's directors or company secretary**

through their contact details at Companies House or telephone directories or through an online search by name.

Landlords

Landlords should carefully consider the legal position and their options. It may not be easy to re-let premises and, in the meantime, empty property rates will be payable by the landlord if they take them back. They may, therefore, want to co-operate with the tenant to try to avoid insolvency. It may even be better to have an insolvent tenant (or the administrator) who is paying the rent, than a void period.

Consider:

- **Is the company whose name is on the lease formally insolvent — or is it another group company? If it is not in administration or liquidation then action for forfeiture or distraint can still be taken.**
- **Are there rent arrears?**
- **When is the next rent day?**
- **Is there a guarantor on the lease?**
- **Is there a rent deposit in hand?**
- **How easy will it be to re-let?**
- **Are there dilapidations to the property?**
- **What form is the insolvency taking?**
- **Is there a chance of a viable business emerging?**
- **Is any former tenant liable for the lease? This may be the case if they assigned the lease to the current or to an intermediary tenant before 1996.**
- **Is there a sub-tenant who may be required to pay rent directly to the landlord?**

Legal advice will be necessary on some of these issues. For example:

- **The precise terms of rent deposit documentation are critical to being able to seize the monies.**
- **The right to pursue a lease guarantor or former tenant can be lost if the landlord takes back the premises. This can be done inadvertently by accepting back the keys or by arranging for prospective tenants to view the premises.**

If a business uses insolvency to escape from a debt, such as a tax liability, and the landlord decides to issue a new lease to the successor company then, unless it is explicitly agreed in the lease, the liability for rent, service charge and dilapidations will be wiped out. It will still be recoverable, in theory, from the original tenant company but it is very unlikely that any payment will result. These debts should be dealt with in negotiations with a successor company.

There may also be an issue regarding the size of debts. If the landlord suffers a small loss of a few hundred or even a few thousand pounds, it may not be worthwhile incurring the expense of legal action to recover it. Even when there is a personal guarantee, it is often not financially worthwhile to pursue debts of less than £10,000. It may be better to preserve a continuing relationship and to write-off such debts and be thankful to still have a tenant.

If the landlord decides to exercise their right to re-enter the property and forfeit the lease then there are two methods.

1. **If the rent is unpaid, the lease will usually permit re-entry without application to the court.**
2. **If the action results from the insolvency being a breach of the lease, a Section 146 notice[34] must be served and a solicitor should be consulted. The administrator may oppose the forfeiture and the court will decide: often the court will require outstanding rent to be paid. Similar considerations may apply in a liquidation. It is important**

---

34 Law of Property Act 1925.

**to act quickly to exercise forfeiture and not enter into
any communication with the tenant that may give the
impression that the lease is continuing: this may act as an
implicit waiver of the right to forfeit.**

An administrator may sell part of a business and grant a licence
to occupy the premises to a new business. The landlord must
decide quickly whether to try to resist this and forfeit the lease
or accept and negotiate a new lease. The key considerations will
be the likelihood of re-letting and the quality of the licensee's
covenant.

What if a landlord becomes insolvent?

The tenant may find that obligations to repair or insure are not
carried out. If the landlord is responsible for servicing of common
parts, these obligations may not be met either. Whilst withholding
the service charge may get the attention of the landlord or
administrator, it may not get the work done and the right of offset
may not be permitted under the terms of the lease. Negotiation
may be necessary to try to restore essential services and this may
call for a pragmatic approach such as paying contractors directly
for these services.

The tenant must check the position on service charge payments
and payments that have been made to the landlord for sinking
funds that are meant to be used to replace assets such as the lift
or to repair the roof. Does the lease specify these sums are held
in trust by the landlord? If there is any doubt then legal advice
may be necessary to prevent an administrator or liquidator
distributing such funds to creditors.

What if the tenant is, in fact, a sub-tenant? If the lease is
forfeited by the intermediary landlord then that could terminate
the tenant's lease. The situation is different if the intermediate
landlord surrenders their lease or a liquidator disclaims it. Legal
advice is essential.

A superior landlord can go to the sub-tenant and serve notice
of arrears of rent from their landlord under the terms of a 1908

Act. This is a complex area that needs legal advice, not least since the law is possibly about to change. The tenant must be careful not to pay any more than the superior landlord specifies. For example, if the tenant usually pays more to his landlord, than he, in turn, pays to the superior landlord; the tenant could mistakenly pay their full rent directly to the superior landlord and still owe their immediate landlord the 'profit rent'. The tenant must be sure to pay the correct person and that the superior landlord is within his rights to demand direct payment.

What if a sub-tenant is in difficulty?

You may be an immediate tenant and have sub-let, with the landlord's consent. Suppose that sub-tenant is in financial difficulty and seeks a change in their lease; the problem is that this may require the consent of the superior landlord.

Employees: what happens, what to do. Pensions.

An administrator or liquidator will make employees redundant, unless they plan to sell part or all of the business as a going concern, when they may keep some or all of the staff. There are occasions when a company will go into solvent administration when it is able to pay its debts. In such circumstances employees will be entitled to their contractual redundancy if that is more generous than the statutory figure. It is more common for a company to be unable to pay its statutory redundancy commitment, in which case the government will step in and pay it.

The order in which people are paid from any available funds is as follows:

- **secured creditors (such as banks);**
- **employees' outstanding pay, holiday pay accrued and redundancy;**
- **tax authorities;**
- **other unsecured creditors.**

The Department for Business, Innovation and Skills (formerly DTI and DBERR) should be able to answer questions. The number to ring is 0845 145 0004 (calls are charged at local rates).

Not everyone is entitled to a redundancy payment. To qualify, you must:

- **have been employed for more than two years for more than 16 hours per week**
- **have been made redundant rather than having your employment terminated for cause;**
- **be below 65 years of age;**
- **not be a director of the business who has a controlling interest — but other directors can claim.**

Calculation of employees' claims in insolvency

Once the total of all the claims has been worked out, the employees can claim directly from the Department for Business, Innovation and Skills (DBIS), which then stands in the employees' shoes and can claim against the company.

If an employer is declared insolvent, cannot or refuses to pay, employees can apply to the DBIS for a direct payment from the National Insurance Fund. But they must have applied in writing to the ex-employer for a payment within six months of the date employment ended, or applied successfully to an employment tribunal within the six months after that.

DBIS will mitigate payments to redundant employees by assuming that they are claiming Job Seekers Allowance. Any pay received in the period between redundancy and claim payment will generally be deducted. So it's probably best practice to make those claims anyway to help relieve financial hardship.

Payments made by the government are subject to maximum 'capped' payments and a week's pay under the Act is currently limited to £380 per week (reviewed annually).

The claims and current statutory limits are as follows:

Arrears of pay

Most people are paid weekly or monthly in arrears. This claim is limited to eight weeks at the statutory limit of £380 per week and includes salaries, wages and sales commissions.

Statutory Notice

Employees are still entitled to statutory notice but if the company is unable to pay, then this is added on to the redundancy claim.

Holiday pay

Limited to six weeks of holiday pay due at the statutory limit of £380 per week or a maximum of £800, in the last 12 months.

Payments in lieu of notice

Under the contract of employment between employer and employee any required notice period due from the employer is payable at the statutory limit of £380 per week.

Redundancy Payments

Redundancy occurs when the employer has ceased or intends to cease the business entirely or in the place where the employee works; or the requirements of that business for the employee to carry out a particular kind of work in that location have ceased or diminished, or are expected to cease or diminish.

Any amount payable is capped at £380 per week. This statutory redundancy payment is calculated by reference to the:

1. **Length of the employee's continuous service at the relevant date;**
2. **The employee's week's pay at the calculation date;**
3. **The employee's age at the relevant date (if they are aged over 64 it is subject to reduction) and during their employment.**

The relevant date would be when statutory notice expires.

If the employee is on piece work, bonuses or variable hours, the average week's pay is calculated from actual earnings in the last 12 weeks of employment.

The maximum number of years to be taken into account for the purposes of calculating a redundancy payment is 20 and the entitlement is:

- **one half week's pay for each complete year in which the employee was less than 22 years old;**
- **one week's pay for each complete year in which the employee was less than 41 but not less than 22 years old;**
- **one and a half week's pay for each complete year of employment in which the employee was 41 years old or more.**

If over 64 years of age, the employees' claim is reduced by one twelfth for each month over 64 so that at the age of 65 there is no payment.

Employees must be able to show two calendar years' continuous employment at the relevant redundancy date, but any period of continuous employment before a worker's eighteenth birthday does not count. Weeks count as weeks of continuous employment if an employee works 16 hours or more or works under a contract normally involving 16 hours' work or more.

Employees' claims rank as a preferential creditor in an insolvency up to the statutory limits set out above. The balance of their claims beyond those limits will rank alongside other unsecured creditors and, in practice, are unlikely to be met in full. Company directors are also eligible alongside other employees.

Employees are sometimes tempted to take things from their insolvent employer as a contribution to what they are owed. This is unlawful and the liquidator could pursue culprits for theft. The assets of the company still belong to the company and will be sold off to pay creditors, of whom the employee is but one. The employee's contract is still in force and should — together with common law — govern their behaviour. As well as having no right of set-off, to seize tangible assets from the company, they also may not take intangible assets such as client lists, software, confidential information etc. They will still have a duty of confidentiality to the company.

CHAPTER 11
BUYING FROM AN ADMINISTRATOR

People buy their own or an unconnected business from an administrator. These are very different situations because, if you have been involved in running the business before administration you know a lot about the people and the detail of how it operates, who its suppliers and customers are etc.

However, there are also issues that affect both types of buyer:

- **If the business will continue to operate from leased premises then confirmation must be obtained that the landlord will transfer the lease. A deal may be made conditional on this or the offer price may be reduced if it cannot be achieved.**
- **Charges over assets that are being acquired must be released before completion of the purchase.**
- **The administrator will not guarantee good title to assets. The purchaser must therefore take a commercial view on these uncertainties and adjust the price accordingly.**

Buying your own business

In theory, employees or directors of a business should know more about its value than any outsider and therefore should be best placed to make a realistic offer for it. An administrator will therefore usually be happy to talk to insiders about making an offer. However, the administrator has a duty to obtain the best price for the assets on behalf of the creditors and will not care who pays as long as it is the highest price. The assets may actually be worth more to a third party than to existing management. On the other hand, the insiders should also be in a position to make a quick offer, because they know the business and don't need to perform any due diligence.

Existing directors and shareholders should use their time advantage to make an offer quickly and to make clear that the offer will be reduced if a deal is not agreed and completed quickly. The directors may have an additional time advantage since they know they are going to appoint an administrator before anyone else does — so they can already have planned what to offer the administrator. They may be in a position to reach a pre-pack deal with the administrator before the actual appointment [see page 131].

If administrators continue to trade the business, it is quite common for them to use the existing management team to manage it in the interim so that it can be sold as a going concern. There will generally be a negotiation over how any profit earned during this period is allocated.

Buying an unconnected business

There are investors who buy businesses from insolvency because they believe they can get a bargain. They may have searched databases or insolvency announcements to find it. Sometimes they will have done business with the company previously or know the directors, employees or shareholders. They may be a customer or supplier whose own business relies upon the insolvent company.

Search strategies include:

• **Internet searches for failed companies, including websites such as http://www.business-sale.com or http://www.ip-bid. com [both accessed 23 August 2011];**
• **reading the *Financial Times* on a Tuesday, when it carries advertisements for the sale of failed companies;**

- getting on the contact lists for insolvency practitioners, telling them what you are looking for so that inappropriate companies are filtered out;
- subscribing to the *London Gazette* where insolvencies must be advertised.

If you are buying a business that you have not previously managed, you need to ask yourself some critical questions:

- **Do you understand the business and its markets?**
- **Why did it fail? Why will you succeed?**
- **What is the deal? Consider the value, which derives from your forecasts and also from the value of assets — you may want to employ an independent valuer. Is payment up-front or partly deferred, with a retention as indemnity for things that could go wrong etc.? Will you buy assets or the business, is anything particular being excluded, will you have access to books and records?**
- **Do you have the necessary management resources?**
- **Do you have the skill to carry out a rapid and effective due diligence?**
- **Are there critical employees and will you retain them?**

Human capital walks out of the door every night and is prone to leave when a business goes into administration. This may include management experience. Existing managers know their way around and can help you get up and running very quickly. They may have the necessary technical skills you need.

- **Are there suppliers and customers critical to the business — and will you retain them?**
- **Do you have sufficient funding in place to complete the purchase, provide working capital and have a reserve to cover the unexpected?**
- **Do you have a team of lawyers and accountants experienced in similar transactions?**

If you buy business assets from an administrator or liquidator they will give no guarantees or warranties because they would be personally liable and because their liability might continue long after the company was wound up. You buy what you see. Therefore if you buy an entire trading business it is up to the buyer to perform due diligence, which involves making enquiries to check that it is as it is believed to be and in the expected condition. There will usually only be a short time for due diligence because the administrator is keen to sell quickly, they want to minimise distractions to staff who are being paid to run the business and there may be other potential buyers competing for the deal. A buyer may make an indicative offer and seek a short period of exclusivity in which to conduct due diligence and complete a deal. This reduces the risk of spending money on an investigation only to find that the administrator sells to someone else. Administrators, on the other hand, are reluctant to agree exclusivity, because they want to be free to sell to any other party who appears. Due diligence will include checking:

- **property rights;**
- **condition of stocks;**
- **condition of machinery;**
- **business data;**
- **employment rights if employees are being taken on.**

The administrator will normally be asked to give an assurance of title — that they have a right to sell what they are selling, and that a third party does not have a claim. However, they will virtually never give a guarantee because they can't be absolutely sure that there is not something they don't know. It may be possible to negotiate paying part of the purchase price into a retention account, repayable in the event of specified problems arising.

They will often be flexible about payment, agreeing to be paid over a period to allow time for assets to be sold and income earned. However, they will probably require security in the meantime.

The purchase deal may not include debtors to the old business, in which case the administrator will often require the purchaser of a business to continue to collect the debtors of the old business, possibly for a commission

Characteristics of purchase from administration

The administrator will be keen to sell quickly because the value of what they have to sell will deteriorate while their costs will increase. If a business is to be sold as a going concern, which will usually deliver the greatest value, they need funds to continue trading. Funds may come from the trading itself, from the sale of some assets or in the form of a deposit from a buyer. Administrators will often prefer a quick sale to the prospect of one at a higher price that is uncertain or delayed. This need for speed reduces the time available for due diligence or for raising finance for a purchase.

After this primary characteristic, others are;

- **Cash — the administrator will prefer immediate cash over the promise of future payments, even if these are higher.**
- **Information — administrators will put together a sales memorandum very quickly but they are not experts on the business. A buyer should try to speak to staff they want to take on, suppliers and customers in order to assess what they will be taking on.**
- **Employees — Under The Transfer of Undertakings (Protection of Employment) Regulations 2006 (TUPE) employees of an insolvent company may automatically transfer to the purchaser with all their previous terms and conditions of employment. Dismissals of staff by the administrators or the company prior to the sale will not necessarily circumvent TUPE, and could give rise to claims against the purchaser for unfair dismissal regardless of any terms in the sale agreement. This is a difficult area of law and depends upon whether the business is sold as a going concern. When the business is sold as a pre-pack, not having**

traded in administration, it is more likely to avoid the TUPE provisions.[35]

- Purchasers should obtain as much information as possible regarding existing and recently dismissed employees. Seek advice as to whether any potential issues arise and, if they do, reflect them in the purchase price or seek an indemnity.

- Landlords — the transfer of business premises to a new owner of the business can be complex and uncertain and will need negotiation with the landlords and legal advice. Landlords cannot be forced to accept a poor quality tenant but, on the other hand, they must not act unreasonably. It is always better to deal with landlords before a purchase, whilst the protection of administration is in place. They may try to get the new occupants to agree to pay the outstanding rent, delaying agreement in the interim. However, they may ask for a rent deposit or other security (such as a personal guarantee) if they agree a transfer, which is not unreasonable, particularly if they lost money in the insolvency, and a deposit may be hard to finance. It may be necessary to conclude a deal with the administrator that is conditional upon agreement with landlords within a specified short time. The conditionality may be that the entire agreement is void if the landlord will not agree or it may just involve a reduction in price. In the period before such an agreement is reached it may be possible to occupy the premises under licence — which is a short-term agreement that confers no rights to continued occupation and no protection under the Landlord and Tenant Act.

- Starting trading — if a new team plan to continue trading a business acquired from administrators they must be prepared for creditors who have lost money to the old business to try to recover some from the new one. They may refuse to supply, demand repayment of old debts, ask for a deposit or change their terms. Suppliers of utility services

---

35 Oakland v Wellswood (Yorkshire) Limited.

such as post, courier, electricity, gas, and telephone will be particularly resistant to continuing service as usual if they believe the business is simply resurrected under a new name. Suppliers may claim retention of title on goods they supplied before administration and the purchase price from the administrator must allow for any successful claims.

Retention of title

Suppliers of goods will often include a term in their terms and conditions of supply that claims they retain title to goods until they have been paid for. This is the so-called Romalpa clause. The law that was expounded by this case sets conditions under which a claim will be successful. The most important is that it must be possible to identify goods that the supplier claims. So a claim will fail if identical goods were supplied by more than one supplier and were not kept separate.

Prohibited trade names

The law restricts the use of a name previously used by a company that has gone into insolvent liquidation. It is designed to prevent companies failing and then starting up again as if nothing had happened as a so-called phoenix company. Directors of the old company are prevented, for five years, from promoting, managing or being directors of a new company trading under the old name (or a very similar one). The prohibition extends to those connected with a new company who follow instructions of a director of the old company. Contravention of these provisions can result in a fine, imprisonment and personal liability for the debts of the new company if it too goes into insolvent liquidation.

However... the law does provide for re-use of the name in certain circumstances:

- **Where an administrator, supervisor in a Company Voluntary Arrangement, or liquidator sells the business as a going** concern to previous directors[36] they may advertise their intention to use the name and circulate all creditors with a copy of the notice [form 4.73 from the government's insolvency website[37]]. This must be done within 28 days of purchase of the business.

- Where it is assets that are sold the new company directors would have to apply to the court for permission to re-use the name. But this provides a second route — application through the courts to reuse a name. If made within seven days of liquidation the name may continue to be used for six weeks or until the date of the court hearing, whichever is earlier. It then needs the permission of the court at that hearing. This is not automatically given. If, for example, the court decides the successor company is not adequately capitalised then it may refuse.
- A director of another company that traded under the name throughout the 12 months prior to liquidation may continue to use it.

I was involved in putting a company into administration and setting up a new company to buy it, except for one branch, which had an onerous lease. We successfully:

- negotiated a transfer of the leases we wanted;
- avoided retention of title claims;
- negotiated new supply with most of our previous suppliers of goods and services;
- arranged for a new bank account and credit card acceptance facilities;
- made employees redundant at the branch we closed before administration;
- retained all our other staff;
- continued trading from retail premises under the previous name.

---

36   Rule 4.228 Insolvency Rules 1986.
37   http://www.insolvency.gov.uk/forms/Form4-73.pdf.

CHAPTER 12
GETTING HELP

When thinking about getting help it is important to think also about the stress involved in financial distress and the loneliness of the situation. It is very difficult to talk to anyone about the problems that are faced. People are reluctant to talk to friends and family about what is happening because of the embarrassment or even shame in having to admit failure. In this situation, friends who are successful are not necessarily the people you want to talk to about your problems because you feel diminished in comparison. It is hard even to discuss these issues with a parent or spouse, and certainly with your children.

However, it is worth making an effort to overcome these barriers because just talking to someone can help to alleviate some of that stress — even if they are unable to make practical suggestions. And decisions made under stress are often the wrong ones. Being able to feel better is therefore an important step towards solving problems.

The people who may be able to offer practical, professional advice include:

- **Your accountant, if you have one. It is easy enough to find an accountant through the recommendation of friends, family or business acquaintances if you don't.**
- **A solicitor will be able to advise on the law, which can be complex in many of the areas touched on in this book. The**

law is also constantly changing, so don't rely on your own knowledge that may be out of date.

- An insolvency practitioner. People will often consult an insolvency practitioner in preference to their accountants because they want the specific expertise they bring, because they think there is no alternative to an insolvency process, or maybe just because they owe money to their accountants that they can't pay. It should be noted that, beyond a brief discussion, the insolvency practitioner is likely to want to be paid an up-front retainer. They are well aware that an insolvent business will not pay their fees.
- Business turnaround specialists may be accountants, solicitors or insolvency practitioners. They may be individuals who are just qualified by experience but, if taking advice from someone who is not qualified, it is important to check the many points of law that may be material.

People who describe themselves as turnaround or business or company rescue specialists fall broadly into three types:

- – Fund managers who are prepared to invest in interesting opportunities.
- – Advisers who will help struggling companies to raise funding from third parties that may include wealthy individuals, banks or investment funds.
- – Advisers whose main focus is in providing practical, legal and strategic advice to businesses to address their problems. They may also help with raising finance but that is incidental to their main focus. They may be accountants, lawyers or insolvency practitioners.
- Licensed administrators.
- The Insolvency Service will not give advice that is specific to an individual case but can provide generic advice.
- The Citizens Advice Bureau can direct enquirers to the relevant sources of advice.

Relevant websites

Website links given below were correct at the time of writing but do note that organisations change responsibilities, merge and close websites. If any of these are not functioning, it may be possible to track their equivalents through a search engine.

Some of the sites are run by commercial organisations. The author has no link to these and cannot guarantee anything about them. They are given to convey an idea about what information is readily available but the reader may do just as well by carrying out their own Internet search.

The UK government's insolvency service provides information via leaflets and its website as well as having statutory responsibilities. Its portal is found at: **http://www.bis.gov.uk/insolvency**
Insolvency service forms: http://www.bis.gov.uk/insolvency/ about-us/forms/england-and-wales

Guidance notes on reuse of company name:
http://www.bis.gov.uk/assets/bispartners/insolvency/docs/ publication-pdfs/reuseofcompanyname.pdf

Leaflet explaining how to make a complaint about an insolvency practitioner:
http://www.bis.gov.uk/assets/bispartners/insolvency/docs/ publication-pdfs/ipcomplaint.pdf

The Department for Business, Innovation and Skills.
This department runs the Enterprise Finance Guarantee Scheme: find out more at http://www.bis.gov.uk/policies/ enterprise-and-business-support/access-to-finance/enterprise-finance-guarantee

Export Credits Guarantee Department:
http://www.ecgd.gov.uk/ [accessed 23 August 2011].
Companies House
This government agency provides information on insolvency, the name of the liquidator of a company, details of companies'

accounts and debentures etc. Much of this information is provided free on the Companies House website or by calling 0303 1234 500, though some information is chargeable.
http://www.companieshouse.gov.uk/about/gbhtml/gpo8.shtml

For tax information

PAYE late payment penalties
http://www.hmrc.gov.uk/paye/problems-inspections/late-payments.htm [accessed 23 August 2011].

HMRC
http://www.hmrc.gov.uk/helpsheets/vas-factsheet.pdf [accessed 23 August 2011].
To research the background of a company and whether it is in financial difficulty
Register of CCJs
http://www.trustonline.org.uk/ [accessed 23 August 2011].

London Gazette
Official newspaper for advertising information relating to insolvencies
http://www.london-gazette.co.uk/ [accessed 23 August 2011].

To find a business adviser or look for a business to buy
Institute for Turnaround may help you find an insolvency practioner or business adviser
http://www.instituteforturnaround.com/
[accessed 23 August 2011].

or the Turnaround Management Association
http://www.tma-uk.org/ [accessed 23 August 2011].

Business sale report
Site that advertises businesses for sale
http://www.business-sale.com/ [accessed 23 August 2011].

Site that advertises businesses for sale
http://www.ip-bid.com/ [accessed 23 August 2011].

Advice on Bailiffs
This site has useful information but it seems to be a commercial
enterprise and charges for more detailed information. Their
email address proved unobtainable, so use the site only with
care.
http://www.bailiffadviceonline.co.uk/index.htm [accessed 23
August 2011].

To find additional finance
Brokers/investors
http://www.beerandyoung.com/the_people.php [accessed 23
August 2011].
http://www.kelsoplace.com/home.stml
http://www.nowfinancialpartners.co.uk/ [accessed 23 August
2011].

Private equity companies
These and companies like them may be able to source
investment in distressed businesses that do have good
prospects if they can overcome short-term difficulties
http://www.valcocapitalpartners.com [accessed 23 August 2011].

Advisory companies
MCR
http://www.mcr.uk.com/index.php [accessed 23 August 2011].
The Company Rescue website also carries quite a lot of helpful
information
http://www.companyrescue.co.uk/ [accessed 23 August 2011].

Litigation Funding (also search litigation finance)
http://www.harbourlitigationfunding.com/ [accessed 23 August
2011].
http://www.calunius.com/ [accessed 23 August 2011].

Relevant legislation:

• Companies Act 2006
• Insolvency Act 1986 (as amended)
• Insolvency Rules 1986 (as amended)
• Insolvency Act 2000
• Council Regulation (EC) No 1346/2000, and
• Enterprise Act 2002.

Note that all liquidators, administrators, administrative receivers and supervisors taking office on or after 29 December 1986 must be authorised insolvency practitioners.

Receiver managers, Law of Property Act (LPA) receivers and nominees appointed to manage a corporate voluntary arrangement moratorium do not have to be authorised.

Insolvency practitioners may be authorised by:

• the Chartered Association of Certified Accountants;
• the Insolvency Practitioners' Association;
• the Institute of Chartered Accountants in England and Wales;
• the Institute of Chartered Accountants in Ireland;
• the Institute of Chartered Accountants of Scotland;
• the Law Society;
• the Law Society of Scotland;
• the Secretary of State for Business, Innovation & Skills.

GLOSSARY

Cash flow	Refers to the movement of cash and bank balances, as distinct from profits, into and out of a business by way of income and payments to suppliers and tax authorities. Its meaning is usually reserved for transactions related to trading but sometimes this is made clear by referring to 'cash flow from trading'.
Companies House	The agency of government that maintains records of companies, directors and charges over company assets.
Completion	As with the purchase of a house, a sale and purchase contract does not complete until all its conditions are satisfied. This may just involve the exchange of money but often there will be other conditions as well.
Due diligence	A process of investigation followed by a purchaser of a business before completing an offer. It usually involves examining records and speaking to staff in order to confirm an understanding of the value of the business and identify any undisclosed liabilities. Purchasers may use their own staff or employ reporting accountants.
Going concern	Describes a business that is able to continue trading as long as there is the prospect of an injection of new funds to return it to solvency. This does not necessarily mean that it is solvent.
Legal person	A company, charity, partnership or association.
Natural person	An individual.

Preferential creditor	Since 2003, when the Enterprise Act 2002 came into force, there are few preferential claims in insolvency. The main remaining ones are; wages owed from the four months before the date of the insolvency (to a maximum of £800), all holiday pay and contributions to occupational pension schemes.
Retention	A sum of money from the purchaser, usually kept in a ring-fenced account by the solicitors acting for the vendor. It is released only when all the conditions specified in the contract have been satisfied. If they are not satisfied then it is returned to the purchaser.
Set-off	Where someone is both a debtor and a creditor to a company, setting the debt against the claim. Depending upon the precise terms of the transactions that have resulted in this situation, there may be no legal right to set one against the other; in which case it may be necessary to pay the debt to the insolvent company even though it also owes you money.
Slow moving stock	Finished goods that may have been in store for some time and that may take a long time to sell relative to other stock.
Shadow director	Someone who is not formally a director but whose instructions, staff and other directors are accustomed to obey.
Working capital	The money required for a business to trade, this is the difference between current assets (comprising stock, debtors and cash) and current liabilities (comprising creditors and short-term loans).

INDEX